# NOT

# MANY

# FATHERS

# NOT MANY FATHERS

## James P. Beck, Jr.
### with Neil Silverberg

**MASTER PRESS**

*an imprint of Morgan James Publishing*

New York

# NOT MANY
# FATHERS

by James P. Beck, Jr.

ISBN: 1-60037-222-8 (Paperback)

**Published by:**

*an imprint of*

Morgan James Publishing, LLC

1225 Franklin Ave. Ste 325

Garden City, NY 11530-1693

Toll Free 800-485-4943

www.MorganJamesPublishing.com

# CONTENTS

# FOREWORD

Writing books has been likened to giving birth to children. Books are not so much written as they are brought forth which accounts for the difficulty of the process. Christian books are no exception. They start with the conception of an idea planted by God, grow through a thought-laden gestation period, and finally are brought forth with much labor and difficulty.

I have been privileged to work alongside the author, Pete Beck, through the entirety of the birthing of this book. From its inception, through the arduous period of perfecting the material, and finally to its completion, it has been obvious that this was a book he was eminently fitted to write. He is so because the birthing of this ma-- terial corresponds to the full blooming of his role as a father in the house of God.

From the moment I first met Pete over twenty-five years ago it was obvious that he carried the welfare of Zion in his heart as only a true spiritual father can. Although pastoring his own church at the time, Pete was attempting to help another church in an entirely different state and I was called along to help. It was evident to me then that God was forming in Pete his own Father-heart. Young men were drawn to him then and he willingly opened his heart to all who came.

Since that initial meeting I have watched with joy the full development of what was then only in its inception. One of the clearest ways in which Pete's role as a father has been evident is his passion to bring leaders together. It was Pete who first conceived the idea of an annual conference to refresh fivefold men from several different streams of New Testament churches. Now in its eleventh year, this unique conference has been greatly used by God to encourage young leaders and provide a setting where young men can see fathers working together. Seeing Pete standing at the lectern each year moderating this unique event has allowed many leaders to see not only his heart for the universal church of God, but also his own growth as a spiritual father.

Since that first conference I have had the privilege of working side by side with Pete in Masterbuilders, a fellowship of New Testament churches. Again, it was in Pete's father-heart that the vision for this group of churches was formed. Observing his care for each of the churches, regardless of size or status, has been an inspiration to all of the team members that work with him.

As Masterbuilders has grown, Pete has been engaged in passing the baton to several younger men around him. In no way has this meant that his own usefulness has been diminished—rather, it has actually grown! Like a father who upon turning his business over to his sons is overjoyed that his sons exceed him, so this has been Pete's joy. His heart continues to beat for the advancement of God's kingdom and in that spirit he has released those around him to find their place in the kingdom of God.

When Pete first posed the idea of writing a book dealing with spiritual fathers, I was excited by the prospect. His own experience over the years has fitted him to speak to the church about this issue. The truths he espouses here were first learned in the anvil of divine experience and are practically fitted for the needs of this present generation.

It is clear that God is speaking to the church in our day regarding the place of fathers in His house. Everywhere you go the subject is on many lips. My own feeling is that this book will contribute much to placing the role of fathers in the proper light. Unless the church in our day comes to terms with the issue of spiritual fathers and learns how to properly relate to them it will remain greatly hindered from realizing its divine destiny.

If there is anything that separates this book from others on the subject it might be in the emphasis it lays on the relationship between churches and spiritual fathers. Too often emphasis is laid on the authority that fathers exercise over churches rather than the relationship they have with those they influence. While fathers certainly are given spiritual authority the proper exercise of that authority can only occur in the context of proper relationships. As many churches have unfortunately discovered, attempting to relate to spiritual authority without healthy relationships can lead to untold damage and difficulty. The exciting thing about this present work is that it not only clearly articulates the need for these relationships, it contains a wealth of practical insights gleaned from many years of experience as a pastor and as one having oversight. I can confidently say that if the truths espoused in this book were properly applied to the relationship between churches and fathers as well as in churches and apostolic networks it would bring great growth of the kingdom of God.

With great joy I commend this present volume to God's people thankful that I have had a part in its production. May the God and Father of our Lord Jesus Christ use the material in this book for His own glory to prepare a generation of fathers to turn their hearts to the children and a generation of children to recognize and honor the fathers among them. May the end result be that the Day of His appearing is hastened. Maranatha!

Neil Silverberg

# ACKNOWLEDGEMENTS

I wish to thank my wife Jane, my son Pete Beck III, and Virginia Malone, Sherri Stevens, Carlton Kenny and Steve Parker, who all gave valuable suggestions to the first manuscript.

I also wish to express my heartfelt gratitude for the excellent help given to me by my friend and co-laborer in Master Builders Fellowship, Neil Silverberg. Neil is a great writer, and without his coaching and editing, I am sure that the final manuscript would have been much poorer. It is not often that one can find someone who selflessly helps educate another in the field of writing. Thank you Neil!

# Part 1

•

## WANTED:

# FATHERS

# 1

# WHY WE NEED FATHERS

For the last several decades there has been a growing emphasis in the church on the restoration of the ministry of the apostle. While some continue to doubt the modern day validity of this ministry, a growing number of churches and church movements have recognized their vital need for this ministry to lead the way as the church approaches the time of the end. As desire has turned to prayer, God has heard and answered by releasing a growing number of true apostles to guide the church in this critical juncture of human history.

While this book does not deal with all aspects of this vital ministry it does focus on what is believed to be the heart of the apostolic office. It is the call of God to be true fathers in the house of God. This call to fatherhood is not limited to the ministry of the apostle for God has called every man and women in the body of Christ to maturity (I John 2:12-14). Relatively few in the church ever seem to advance to that place. Yet for those who are rightly called "apostles," such maturity is crucial. We shall see that much damage has been done by those in apostolic ministry who have not allowed the maturity of fathers to be the basis of their ministry.

When I speak about God giving the church fathers I am not speaking in a general sense about those who are teachers, preachers, or leaders. Thankfully, we have not had a shortage of gifted men who could minister to the church. When we speak of fathers we are talking about God giving to the church more than gifted men. Fathers are those who have the heart of God for the church, who live not for their own blessing and purpose, but that God's people might be fully blessed. We are talking about men who fully share the Father's great heart and through whom God can bring the children to maturity.

The Scriptures have much to say about spiritual fathers and their importance to the people of God. To understand this we will not limit ourselves to the New Testament. For spiritual fathers did not appear with the death and resurrection of Christ and the creation of the Body of Christ. Even among God's people in the Old Testament there were spiritual fathers who played an important part in leading the nation of Israel. Under both covenants God has ordained spiritual fathers as an integral part of the life of God's people.

## The Chain of Causation

Before the nation of Israel was officially founded at the exodus, a microcosm of God's plan for was revealed with the fathers. God entered into a special agreement with the fathers of Israel in which He promised to do certain things for their descendants after them. The basis of all that God would do therefore for Israel originated with this covenant with the fathers.

On the eve of Israel inheriting the land of Canaan, Moses reminded their descendants why it is that God had delivered them from Egypt and gave them this good land:

> "Because he loved your fathers and chose their descendants after them, he brought you out of Egypt by his Presence and his great strength, to drive out before you nations greater and stronger than you and to bring you into their land to give it to you for your inheritance, as it is today. Acknowledge and take to heart this day that the Lord is God in heaven above and on the earth below. There is no other. Keep his decrees and commands, which I am giving you today, so that it may go well with you and your children after you and that you may live long in the land the Lord your God gives you for all time." (Deuteronomy 4:37-44)

Notice how Moses clearly reminds Israel that these blessings were not due to anything that they had done or will ever do. Rather, their present blessings began with the fact that God loved their fathers! The chain of God's incredible purpose for Israel begins with His love for the fathers. And because He loved them He chose their descendants after them, promising to give them the land they were to inherit. This is not to say that God does not also love the children, for God is love! His incredible love is not reserved for the fathers only, but it is singled out and emphasized in this scripture.

The fathers spoken of here were the patriarchs of the Israelite nation, Abraham, Isaac, and Jacob. God's plan for the nation began with these three men and the covenant that He made with them. That covenant contained promises that would endure to every generation of their descendants. Even today, that covenant is in effect as evidenced by the fact that the descendants are still receiving the blessing.

God loved the fathers and therefore was wonderfully blessing their descendants! We can establish from this that God's plan to bless His people (and through them the world) always begins with His love for fathers. When God begins to unfold His plan he first looks for those who are fathers to initiate His purpose. For this reason he has the highest regard for those who are fathers.

Because God loved their fathers we should not be surprised to find that he instilled in the consciousness of their descendants the absolute importance of honoring them. Even the simple command to honor their earthly fathers is an expression of that. This is why the Decalogue contains the clear command:

> "Honor your fathers and mothers, so that it might be well with you" (Ex 20:12).

The basis of this command is to be found in the incredible value God placed on fathers. And Israel was to understand that to value what God valued would be the means of great and ultimate blessing. As each Israelite honored their earthly fathers God would bless them in very measurable ways. So important was this command that their very well being depended on it. If they obeyed it they were promised God's blessings; if they did not they could expect no blessing.

## A Divine Principle

This call to honor fathers is not just an archaic command for ancient Israel. It is a divine principle applicable to the people of God in every age. That is why even in the New Testament we find the command to honor fathers repeated again, but with the added promise for those who obey it that they would "prosper and live long on the earth" (Ephesians 6:2). It is interesting to note that this instruction is found in that section of Ephesians where the apostle demands the highest ethical behavior among those who call themselves saints. What must be remembered is that prior to this section (chapters four through six), Paul has been teaching that "through the church, the manifold wisdom of God should be made known to the rulers and authorities in the heavenly realms" (Ephesians 3:10). We must take this wonderful statement at face value. The great mystery of the ages is that the unseen realm gazes intently at the church because through her they are being instructed in the wisdom of God.

It stands to reason therefore that the chapters that follow (four through six) relate to the carrying out of His wisdom referred to in Ephesians 3:8. Included in that section is the command to honor fathers. More than an ethical injunction, as the church obeys this word and honors its fathers it is moving in that wisdom of God by which the unseen realm is instructed in the ways of God. So behind this command to honor fathers lies the church's ability to fulfill its ultimate role as the vehicle through which the unseen realm learns the wisdom of God.

In First Corinthians, the apostle Paul reminds his converts that he alone has the authority to bring correction to them since his relationship to them is more than that of a teacher (I Corinthians 4: 15). This passage reveals the heart of real apostolic ministry. Paul speaks to his "father" relationship with the church at Corinth as the basis of his appeal and the exercise of his authority. He expected them to understand that while God had blessed them with many gifted men, they had only one father in the faith. This establishes the important principle that fathers are not just gifted individuals, but those who have a special relationship with churches on the basis of their having brought them faith. Since the Corinthian church existed as a result of Paul's coming to them, he alone held the unique role of being their father. That being the case they were duty bound to receive from him in a way they should not from any other teacher.

We must remember that all of the churches in the New Testament were "first generation churches," that is, started by the apostles. As the faith rapidly spread throughout the earth there would be many churches which would emerge through various means other than apostolic witness. Because of this, some of these churches would be in need of fathers as well. As we shall discover later, many of these churches would find relationship with apostolic men who may not have been the vehicle through whom the church came into being. This is important for understanding how many churches today are relating to fathers who are not the ones that actually started their church. Nevertheless, true fathers have earned the respect in, and are adopting these churches in order to provide them with the blessing of fatherhood.

## A Fatherless Generation

We have seen that in both the Old and New Testaments fathers held a vital place in the life of God's people. But how should the modern church relate to fathers? Are they needed in today's church? And if so how do churches go about finding fathers they can relate to?

We should begin by recognizing that besides being solidly biblical, there is an important reason that fathers are desperately needed in the Church in our day. The Church, like the culture in which it exists, has become increasingly fatherless. The absence of true fathers has meant that a major source of strength and blessing has been absent from the church.

There is no need to cite statistics to prove that our culture is suffering from a lack of input from fathers. The evidence is all around us. Besides a skyrocketing divorce rate, studies show that even in homes where the two parent family is in tact, the actual time that fathers spend with their children has been steadily diminishing. This is due in part to expanded work schedules and an increasing prosperity which has only fostered the idea that children only need more and more things. Many fathers have consigned themselves to giving their families more and more material things while withdrawing from the daily input that only a father can give.

Unfortunately, this lack of involvement by fathers in the family today seems to have its counterpart in the church as well. There has been a noticeable absence of real fathers in our churches and we have been feeling the effects for a long time. There are numerous reasons for this. Perhaps the chief one has been an occupation with doing instead of being. We continue to believe in the Western church that maturity can be measured by how busy we are. No wonder we have produced few fathers. Fathers are not those whose effectiveness is measured by how busy they are, but by their relationship with others. And this is just the problem. Many of those who by now should be fathers have been so busy with ministry that they have had little or no time to relate to those they should be training!

## Story of a Leader

In my early days, I sat under the leadership of a very charismatic man whose ministry blessed many people. He was a natural leader with many gifts. People readily followed him, including several other strong leaders. When he died unexpectedly a real vacuum was created. Some of the young men who had been with him tried to immediately fill the gap. Unfortunately, none of these young men had either the anointing or the gifts of this particular brother, nor his strong charismatic personality. They only had his example or role model of leadership. So when the time came for someone to replace him these men tried nobly, but none could fill his shoes.

What soon became apparent was that these men had not sat under a father, but under a young man (I John 2:13-14) in that they were all achievers and fighters and doers, like the man they had followed. One of God's fundamental laws is that like engenders like. Young men, according to John, are strong and have overcome the Devil. This speaks of activity and doing rather than being. A father, on the other hand, is concerned with being and understanding one's position in Christ. A father is one who has "known Him Who is from the beginning." This speaks of rest. They are more apt to rest in God.

My friend had not adequately prepared men to fill his shoes upon his departure. Indeed he could not, for he himself was a young man and could not bring those around him any further than he himself had gone. Like begets like. This was evident in the continued air of independence and spiritual pushing and shoving among the brethren, hindering any progress towards unity among men and churches. A tremendous amount of time was wasted. It took years of waiting on the Holy Spirit to sort things out and do some breaking in many hearts (including mine) before the situation could be built upon by the Holy Spirit. We learned through this that a whole lot more than just dynamic leadership is needed to insure the future of a church or movement. A father's anointing and role modeling is needed as well.

This same scenario has been repeated again and again in many churches and church movements. While a gifted leader is alive he may gather around him a certain following. During his lifetime his own giftings and abilities may impart a measure of stability and blessing to his followers. But what happens if he suddenly dies or is unable to continue his ministry due to sickness or moral failure? We have often seen the unfortunate results of such a situation. In some churches it has meant a continuing power struggle among leaders and church members or worse, a church split.

All of this probably could have been avoided if the individual leading that church or church movement had been a mature father who understood his role as that of adequately preparing the next generation of leaders. By this I mean raising up fathers in his place, not just ministry. This does not guarantee a smooth transition, but does insure ultimate success. Instead of gathering a following around himself based solely on his own giftedness, such a leader would be looking to gather around him a generation of sons who would become fathers also and who would continue his work when he was gone. But none of us understood this at the time. We all, including my departed friend, did the best we could with what we understood at that time of our lives. I am so glad that the Lord does not hold our past ignorance against us. But now the Holy Spirit is revealing a new dynamic.

## Giant Killers

The story of Saul, Israel's first king contains much instruction regarding the importance of fathers. Saul, whose reign was a total failure was called to be a spiritual father to the nation of Israel. Unfortunately Saul was unwilling to cooperate with God and instead of being a father ended up resisting the very thing that God was doing in the nation.

One of the evidences that Saul failed as a father was that his men never killed a single giant! That was because Saul never killed any, and he was their role model. Only one of his subjects, David, ever killed a giant. Initially, Saul tried to discourage him, but finally let him try. Then he spent the rest of his life trying to kill the giant killer, the one man who was worth mentoring!

David's men killed several giants in 2 Samuel 21. This occurred when David was old and succumbing to physical weakness. He was still out there trying however. His men came to the rescue and the chapter records how they killed several giants. This is a perfect picture of how young men take after their role models. To produce a giant killer, you have to be one. To produce a father, you have to be one.

This brings us to an important description of the role of fathers in the church today. Fathers are those who are always primarily looking for and improving relationships with sons, to train them and release them to carry on their work when they are gone. True fathers therefore, are those with a long-range view of things, looking beyond their own generation to those who will be around when they have departed . And they are not merely looking at the next generation; they are doing everything they possibly can to equip that generation to go further than they did in their own day, both by teaching and setting an example, by being a role model.

This is an important point. Fathers are characterized as those who desire their sons to do better than they did. This is not difficult to understand. If I have a business in which I am training my son to take over, do I want him to do as well as I? If I am a real father will I want my son to do merely as well as I did? My real desire should be that he surpass me in every way! That he would increase the family inheritance! That is a natural desire of my father-heart and I will make every provision for him to better me.

The same is true of spiritual fathers. They are those in the church who are literally "giving themselves away" so that their sons around them may succeed. We must settle in our hearts right away that this call to be a father is a call to the most selfless place there is. If we are still looking out for ourselves, seeking praise and authority, then we have not captured the heart of a father.

# 2

# MAKING KNOWN THE FATHER

The restoration of fathers in the Church today is vital to the fulfillment of God's purpose in the earth. Let's review:

> "See, I will send you the prophet Elijah before that great and dreadful day of the Lord comes. He will turn the hearts of the fathers to their children, and the hearts of the children to their fathers; or else I will come and strike the land with a curse."

As the time of His reappearing approaches, the importance of fathers in the Church will become quite clear. We simply will not realize the fullness of God's plan for the Church without the presence of many fathers to lead the way.

In the previous chapter we began to understand who these spiritual fathers are and why they are so important to the church. It is vital that we have a clear perception of this call to spiritual fatherhood. Only then can we properly understand how these spiritual fathers function in God's house today. In this chapter we will continue to shed light on what Scripture says about spiritual fathers.

## Why Did Jesus Come?

Perhaps the best place to start in understanding spiritual fathers is by asking the simple question, "Why did God send His Son into the earth?" The most obvious answer is that He came into the world in order to die and by His death redeem mankind. This is basic New Testament teaching regarding the first coming of Jesus. Even Jesus Himself referred to His death as the ultimate purpose of His coming. Prior to the start of his ministry, John the Baptist looked upon and called Him the "Lamb of God, who takes away the sin of the world!" (John 1:29). It is clear from Scripture that Jesus Christ was born to die and to give His life a ransom for many."

Yet while this is true it still leaves us with an important question: "If Jesus' death was the only reason for His coming into the world why did He live for thirty-three years upon the earth? Why wasn't He simply sacrificed soon after He was born or as a young man? This is not a moot question but goes to the very heart of why the Son came. And the answer is that while His death was the means of redeeming a sinful world, it was through his Life that He fully revealed the Father. In other words, Jesus came not only to die for the sins of the world, but that through Him the Father might be fully revealed.

Jesus testified to this during His earthly ministry:

All things have been delivered to Me by My Father, and no one knows who the Son is except the Father and who the Father is except the Son, and the one of whom the Son wills to reveal Him. Then He turned to His disciples and said privately, 'Blessed are the eyes which see the things you see.' (Luke 10:22-23)

Then they said to Him, "Where is your Father?" Jesus answered. "You know neither Me nor My Father. If you had known Me, you would have known My Father also." (John 8:19)

"I and my Father are one." (John 10:30)

If you had known Me, you would have known My Father also; and from now on you know Him and have seen Him. Philip said to Him, "Lord, show us the Father, and it is sufficient for us. Jesus said to him, "Have I been with you so long, and yet you have not known Me, Philip? He who has seen Me has seen the Father; so how can you say, 'Show us the Father'? (John 14:7-9)

All of these passages reflect this vital aspect of the coming of Jesus into the earth. It also explains all that He did during the three years of His earthly ministry. Why did Jesus spend much of his time healing the sick and delivering men and women from demon possession? There is only one answer. Since the Father is merciful and compassionate, Jesus manifested that compassion by healing the sick and casting out demons. When Jesus raised men from the dead and gave them life He did so precisely because the Father raised the dead and gave them life. The entire earthly ministry of Jesus therefore can be summed up by simply saying that Jesus came to earth to demonstrate to mankind what His Father was really like. And to a world blinded by sin this was an absolute necessity.

This being the case, it is very instructive to see that Jesus constantly addressed God as His Father during His earthly life. In point of fact, He used the Aramaic term for father which when translated into the modern vernacular is equivalent to our English term daddy. This was, of course, not the typical way that Jews of His day referenced God. What we must remember is that Jesus did so against the backdrop of centuries of Old Testament history in which God had revealed Himself as Jehovah, the Old Testament covenant name of God. That name Jehovah was usually joined to another word giving the Hebrew people a window into the nature of the God who had saved them. For instance, Jehovah Jireh (the Lord our provider) and Jehovah Shamah (the Lord is there) both revealed aspects of God's Person and His relationship to His covenant people. Other names such as Adonai (Lord) and El Shaddai (God Almighty) also revealed something important to the covenant people about their God. When Jesus appeared there is no record of his referring to God by any of these covenant names at all. Then what did He mean by saying He had revealed God's name to His disciples?

> "And now, O Father, glorify Me together with Yourself, with the glory which I had with You before the world was. I have manifested your name to the men whom You have given Me out of the world. They were yours, You gave them to Me, and they have kept your word" (John 17:5-6)

Is there a specific name used by Jesus by which He revealed God to His disciples? Searching the Gospels carefully we discover that the primary name that Jesus called God was simply that of Father. This is the primary way that He referenced God to those who were His closest friends on earth.

It is important to remember that in Scripture there is a close relationship between a name and the person who bears it. The name is the person revealed and the name is the person actively present.[1]

The name "Father" therefore is more than an appellation—it provides us with the ultimate description of Who God is. Simply stated, God is above all else a father. When Jesus came to earth He came to fully manifest the Father to us. And in that name we find the most complete revelation of the living God ever given to mankind.

Jesus chose to use this name for God for good reason. It is only by understanding that God is Father that we are able to grasp His purpose in the earth. The entire plan of God is bound up in that name! Why? Because when we refer to God as Father we are speaking of that which He purposed in the beginning before He ever created the earth and placed men and women on it. It is in understanding God as Father that His unique plan finds its origin.

## The Proper Place to Start

When we speak of God as Father we are talking about God in His supreme role. The fact that He is a Father governs all of His holy activity. Is He Creator? Sustainer? Provider? Yes, indeed God is all of these things, but they essentially describe what He does in relation to His creation, not Who He is. If we want to talk about Who He really is we must say that He is first and foremost Father. And knowing Him as such is the only way to accurately understand what He has purposed.

During His earthly ministry, Jesus not only referred to His present relationship with His Father, He alluded to the relationship He had with the Father in eternity past as well. This comes out clearly in what is known as the priestly prayer in the seventeenth chapter of John's Gospel. While praying before the disciples, Jesus spoke of the "glory you have given me because you loved me before the creation of the world" (John 17:24). This prayer affords us a small glimpse into the relationship between the Father and the Son that existed even before Creation.

What these and other passages reveal is that God was a Father before He ever created Adam and Eve and entered a relationship with them. That should raise an interesting question. If He was a Father in eternity past who were His children? The answer is that He was first the "God and Father of the Lord Jesus Christ" before He became our Father through the miracle of regeneration. Even though the Father and Son were one in essence, in the Godhead they maintained a "father and son" relationship. His relationship to God as Father therefore did not just begin on earth. It was an expression of the relationship that the Son enjoyed with the Father before Creation in the Godhead. There is great mystery attached to this but it is clearly spoken of in Scripture.

Where then do we come in? What is clear is that in eternity past the Father initiated a plan to expand His divine family. Through the agency of His Son He would bring into existence a race of sons all bearing the image of His lovely Son. That is exactly why in his translation of the New Testament epistles, J.B. Phillips translated Ephesians chapter one and verse four this way: "Before eternity God determined to bring into existence a race of sons." Phillips caught the essence of the divine plan to have a vast company of [2]sons. This entire first chapter of the book of Ephesians provides us with a wonderful window into this incredible divine mystery. Throughout this chapter, the apostle Paul constantly refers to the Father as the origin of the divine plan. In fact, the Father is the main subject of almost every verb in the chapter! From the beginning, the Father had a plan to include this wonderful creation called Man in the fellowship that existed between the Father and the Son. This is the reason for the creation of Earth and the unique race capable of entering into the fellowship of the Father and the Son.

What seems clear from this passage is that the divine plan was not conceived by the Father as a knee jerk reaction to the Fall. As we have seen, it was conceived "before the creation of the world" (1:4). Obviously, that predates the Fall itself. Because man is fallen it would necessitate the Son's coming to earth in order to die to redeem fallen man, yet that is not the main focus of the plan. From the beginning, the divine plan in the heart of the Father was to bring into existence a race of sons all patterned after His own unique Son. Because they are fallen they must first be redeemed, but redemption is not the central reason for bringing these sons into existence.

## The Sons Share Life

Scripture goes further in describing the relationship between Father and Son by pointing out that Father and Son also share the same life:

> For as the Father has life in Himself, so He has given to the Son to have life in Himself (John 5:26)

This passage provides us with a glimpse into the mystery of the triune God. Jesus alludes to the fact that both He and the Father possess this life in themselves; it is not derived from any other source. Theologians are accustomed to referring to this aspect of the divine nature as "self-existence." The life these Scriptures speak of is not just natural life, which human beings share with all other creatures, but divine life. The fact that the Father and the Son share this life is the basis for the unique fellowship that exists between them. This fellowship began in eternity past and continued on when Jesus left glory and came to earth.

As we have already seen, it was the Father's good purpose to bring into existence an extended family and inviting them into the same fellowship He enjoyed with His Son (I John 1:1-3). Since divine life was the basis of that fellowship it would require that each of the sons receive that life and thus become His children. That is why Scripture presents salvation, not only in terms of receiving the forgiveness of sins, but sharing of divine life as well (II Cor. 5:17, II Peter 1:3, I John 5:12). This is what Jesus means when he tells Nicodemus "you must be born again"[3] (John 3:3). The very life that both the Father and Son shared in themselves would through procreation now become the basis of the life of the children of God. Therefore when the children of God call Father, it is not a mere appellation, but a confession that they have now come into possession of divine life or as Scripture calls it "eternal life."

It is critical to see the priority that God places on life. Wherever God manifests Himself there is the presence of life. This life was the basis of everything in the beginning (John 1:4). God is a God of life and when He manifests Himself there is life.

We are living in a time when the modern world is preoccupied with discovering the origins of life. Recently, scientists announced that after many years of trying they have successfully mapped out the entire genetic code of human DNA. This genetic map is the first step in allowing modern man to control such things as the sex of a newborn, and the ability to predict certain propensities for disease. These discoveries have only strengthened man's resolve to "be as God"—not only understanding the mystery of life, but being able to create it as well. The implications of this are incredible and the debate is only now beginning.

Of course, man's preoccupation with discovering the origins of life pertains only to the physical side of things. Unregenerate man knows nothing of the Spirit side of life. It is to the Church alone that God has given the privilege of partaking of divine life. And it is only as we understand this that we can properly understand how God intends the Church to function.

# Life in the Church

Since the Church is the company of those who have received divine life, it must be built up by that same life. Perhaps the best way to understand this is by using the term "organic" to describe the life of the church. By 'organic' we mean that it is something alive because it possesses life.

The alternative to organic is 'mechanic.' What we mean when we say that something is mechanic is that it is animated by means of a certain mechanism by which it is able to duplicate some of the actions of a human. A robot, for instance, might be programmed to make the same movements as a human being on an assembly line. But making the same movements does not mean that the robot possesses life, for it does not. The animating life principle of the robot is mechanical—it is programmed to act a certain way and cannot act otherwise. The opposite is true of that which is organic. It lives and moves simply because it possesses life.

Failure to recognize the organic nature of the church will hinder us from being able to build her up. Yet many churches have no understanding of the organic nature of body of Christ. Bereft of understanding as to her true nature, they treat the church mechanically equating busy church programs for the presence of life. Others perpetuate age-old traditions devoid of spiritual life. God help us when programs and structures become a substitute for the anointing of Christ (life) in our churches!

What we want and need is real life in our churches. Those of us who want to go on and fulfill the end time destiny of the church desperately want real life to be manifested. Divine life will attract men who are now living in death. Throughout the land today prophets are speaking of a worldwide harvest of souls ready to be reaped before the Lord's appearing. This will necessitate the presence of life in our churches. We have mistakenly assumed that this harvest will be reaped by means of certain methods or programs. It will not. The church in the end of days will be a Church that possesses divine life and that manifests that life. And because of that life it will be a church which produces many fathers who in turn will beget many sons.

## Fathers and Life

What does all of this have to do with fathers in the church? It has much to do with it. It is only as we understand the primacy of life in the church that we will recognize the importance of fathers. For in a real sense, fathers are those who are characterized by two things: intimate fellowship with the Father so that they share His viewpoint, and the ability to impart life to others. We will look at both of these in the remainder of this book.

The apostle John describes fathers as those who "know Him Who is from the beginning" (I John 2:14). The reference to knowing Him Who is from the beginning means that fathers are those who possess a knowledge of God rooted in His eternal purpose. They have understood God's intention to have a vast family of sons "attaining to the whole measure of the fullness of Christ" (Eph. 4:13).

Yet what makes them fathers is that they themselves have begotten offspring. They can initiate or impart life! The whole issue of divine life in the church means that God must have those who are able to produce a spiritual progeny—sons who will themselves be able to watch and appreciate fatherly role models, become fathers themselves and impart life to others. Spiritual fathers are the only means of preserving a true work of God beyond a particular generation.

1 See an excellent discussion of the Bible effect of a name on pages 862-864 in The New Bible Dictionary. William B. Eerdmans Publishing Co, Grand

Rapids Michigan, 1974, Edited by J.D. Douglas. The article was written by J.A. Moyyer, M.A.BD. Vice Principal of Clifton Theological College, Bristol, England.

2. By using the male gender term "sons" the Bible is not excluding females. It is a generic term by which all of the children of God are referred to. Elsewhere Paul says that "we are all sons of God through Jesus Christ" (Galatians 3:26).

3 The word translated "again" in John 3:3 could also be translated "from above." In fact, this seems to be the best English translation of the term. In His conversation with Nicodemus, Jesus is not referring to time, but to place of origin. Those who are born of God are "born from above" that is, heaven is not just the place of destiny, but of origin as well.

# 3

# FATHERHOODS

In the New Testament, the relationship of God as Father applies
only to believers. While God is said to be a Father to all men in a
general sense based on creation, the idea of a redeeming fatherhood
of God to all men is not mentioned. As a matter of fact, Jesus speaks
rather pointedly to the quibbling Jews, "You are of your father, the
Devil." (John 8:44). It is really only in respect to the "new" life, or
life from above, i.e., the new birth, that the redeeming fatherhood
of God applies. We shall explore this thought more thoroughly in
this chapter. Those who read the King James Version of the Bible

have undoubtedly come across that archaic word "begat" in the early chapters of Genesis as well as in Matthew's Gospel. It is found in those long genealogical lists containing the record of certain descendants of certain men. No doubt we have often skipped over these long genealogical lists when reading through Genesis or Matthew. Or perhaps we have found them to be effective sedatives when finding it difficult to fall asleep.

The modern translations replace "begat" by simply saying that "Isaac became the father of Jacob" or, "Abraham was the father of Isaac." While it says essentially the same thing it does so by avoiding the use of the archaic begat. Dropping the use of the word the sentence is framed in what is called the passive form. Contrarily, when begat is inserted the statement takes on what is known as the active sense. That's because begat is an active word which speaks of initiation. Webster's Dictionary defines begat as a verb meaning "to procreate, usually said of the father: to cause." When we look up the word procreate Webster defines it simply as the "production of offspring."

In human procreation it is the father who initiates. The mother receives and nurtures and brings to bear, but the conception of a new life is dependent upon an initiatory act of a father. It implies that a man went into his wife and in the normal course of events a child was the outcome. In this chapter we want to talk of the importance of this act of initiation in producing new life. This will help us to understand this entire concept of fatherhood in Scripture.

## The Old Testament Promise of Life

The Old Testament begins with the story of the creation of the first man, Adam, through whom all men and women derive their life. In a real sense, he is the "father of the human race." This means that humanity not only derives its physical existence from Adam, but its spiritual existence as well.

After Eve had yielded to the tempter and eaten of the forbidden fruit along with her husband, human beings experienced a radical fall from their previous state. This fall meant that death now worked in them physically and spiritually. This death was now to be passed on to all their descendants through the normal process of procreation. That is why the Word of God teaches that "in Adam all men die." (I Corinthians 15:22)

Yet immediately after the Fall God promised to send the "Seed of the woman" to undo its disastrous effects (Genesis 3:15). This is commonly regarded as the fountainhead of all Messianic prophecy in Scripture since it sets in motion the process of selecting a certain progeny through whom the Christ would spring. All of God's work in human history from this point on was to select and carefully preserve the seed until the descendant who would redeem humanity from the curse of the Fall would come and "bruise the serpent's head."

This promise of a seed might be properly called the "promise of life" (II Timothy 1:1). Just as from Adam all men derive the negative effects of the Fall, so God purposed that through one family line, life might be passed to all. The family line of the "seed" begins with the selection of Seth whose genealogy is carefully preserved in Genesis five. It is interesting to note that in the previous chapter there is a history of the family line of Cain, the one rejected in favor of Abel (who was replaced by Seth). Yet upon inspection, we discover that the Cainite record is characteristically different than that of Seth. It simply lists a number of Cain's descendants, but is completely lacking any information about them. When we compare it to the Sethite genealogy we discover that there is much more information about each descendant of Seth's family line. This is because the Scriptures focus upon the preservation of this one family through whom the promise of Divine Life would be fully realized.

The Sethite chronology contains a record of seven generations until the appearance of Noah. While it is true that all present day human beings derive their life from Adam it is equally true that all spring from Noah. After the Flood the entire human race was divided up between his three sons. That means that all of the color and racial genes from Adam and Eve were present in those three sons of Noah and the four matriarchs, their wives. Yet Noah passed on more than a physical heritage to these sons—he also carried in his loins the promise of life which he passed to his youngest son, Shem. The prophecy of Noah to Shem after he awoke from his drunken stupor makes it clear that this one of son of Noah carried in his loins the divine promise.

So in this story of human beginnings in Genesis and especially that of the history of the Seed, we learn the important truth that "life is in the seed." It is God's intention that each generation of fathers pass on the promise to their seed in their prospective generations. For the Sethite line this meant that not only did each father pass on his fallen human nature to his progeny (Genesis 5:1), but the promise of life as well. Life came down through Seth.

## Fatherhood in the New Testament

In the New Testament the apostle Paul makes a profound statement regarding the purpose of his ministry:

> "and to make all men see what is the fellowship of the mystery, which from the beginning of the ages has been hidden in God who created all things through Jesus Christ" (Ephesians 3:9)

Speaking about this fellowship of the mystery and the purpose of the church, he follows with this extremely important thought.

"His intent was that now, through the church, the manifold wisdom of God should be made known to the rulers and authorities in the heavenly realms, according to his eternal purpose which he accomplished in Christ Jesus our Lord. In him and through faith in him we may approach God with freedom and confidence. I ask you, therefore, not to be discouraged because of my sufferings for you, which are your glory. For this reason I kneel before the Father, from whom his whole family in heaven and on earth derives its name" (Eph. 3:10-15)

In the original Greek text the word translated "family" is literally the word, fatherhoods. Therefore the verse should read, "For this reason I kneel before the Father, from whom all the fatherhoods in heaven and on earth derives their name." This is important since it tells us that there are fatherhoods in heaven and earth. We can see the connection between this word and the concept of family. A family is created through a father by means of procreation.

We can see how this was true of the fathers of the nation of Israel, the patriarchs Abraham, Isaac, and Jacob. Through them the nation had its physical beginnings. Yet today, this idea of fatherhood has a much wider application than merely the physical. It is also used in a general sense for anyone who conceives something and brings it into being. In this sense, father is a word used of a whole host of people from politicians to founders of industry. We still refer to George Washington as the "father" of our country. It is written that God made Joseph a "father" to Pharaoh (Genesis 45:8). Orville and Wilbur Wright are rightly called the "fathers" of modern aviation since they are attributed with being the founders of it. Simon Bolivar is often referred to as the "father" of several South American nations.

One of the key things to note about this is that a man is said to be a 'father' when what he initiates continues to exist. No one today would say that Teddy Roosevelt is the father of the 'Bull Moose' Party for that political party no longer exists. A father is one who initiates something (a family, an industry, a nation, a church) that continues after he is gone. A 'fatherhood' means the beginning of some kind of life or vision that was initiated through an individual and continues to this day.

## Churches Have Fathers

As with nations and political systems churches are initiated by fathers as well. A church is founded by God's anointing, gifting, and vision imparted through a person. The life of the Father is imparted to someone which in turn creates vision in that individual. This is imparted to others and often the result is that a church comes into being.

We often refer to such a person as a pioneer: one willing to plow ahead and break new ground. Our own nation was founded by such pioneers: men and women with vision to move away from territory already settled in search of new lands. Because of their vision they often inspired others to launch out with them. The result was that many areas of our own country, especially in the West, were discovered and the country rapidly grew.

Churches are often started by such pioneers. This was especially true of those first generation churches started by the apostles in the New Testament. These apostles were men who shared the Father's heart and life who gave birth to new spiritual families. That is why the apostle was essentially the church planter in the First Century. The principle of life is in the father and as life flows through him things are initiated.

In appealing to the Church at Corinth who were rejecting his apostolic authority, Paul reminds them of how he became their spiritual father:

"For it seems to me that God has put us apostles on display at the end of the procession, like men condemned to die in the arena. We have been made a spectacle to the whole universe, to angels as well as to men. We are fools for Christ, but you are so wise in Christ! We are weak, but you are strong! You are honoured, we are dishonoured! To this very hour we go hungry and thirsty, we are in rags, we are brutally treated, we are homeless. We work hard with our own hands. When we are cursed, we bless; when we are persecuted, we endure it; when we are slandered, we answer kindly. Up to this moment we have become the scum of the earth, the refuse of the world. I am not writing this to shame you, but to warn you, as my dear children. Even though you have ten thousand guardians in Christ, you do not have many fathers, for in Christ Jesus I became your father through the gospel. Therefore I urge you to imitate me. For this reason I am sending to you Timothy, my son whom I love, who is faithful in the Lord. He will remind you of my way of life in Christ Jesus, which agrees with what I teach every-where in every church." (I Corinthians 4:9-17) Emphasis mine.

The apostle begins by referring to himself and the other apostles as "last of all," a clear reference to all the persecution and difficul-ties they often endured. For Paul, these things were not a cause of shame, but the very basis of his credentials as an authentic apostle. True apostles must suffer these things (from the world, not the church) and therefore the Corinthians should not be ashamed of Paul for his sufferings. Paul speaks this way though, because that is exactly what has happened. The church at Corinth had been seduced by super-apostles who had succeeded in convincing them that these very difficulties Paul endured were evidences he was not an apostle. In their minds, a true apostle would never suffer these things.

Paul then bases his appeal on the fact of his relationship to them as a 'father' (vs. 15). It was he who had first come to them with the Gospel (see Acts 18). This is the principle of initiation previously referred to. He is their father because he is their apostle—without him they wouldn't exist! Because Paul had begotten them, they were his sons and therefore they should honor him.

The apostle further reveals his father-heart in his reference to sending Timothy who would remind them of everything Paul himself would say in person. Here we see another aspect of a father. Sons are called to be faithful to that which they have received from fathers so that it may be carried on to others. We shall talk later about the tremendous blessing that occurs when this actually happens (see chapters 4 and 5). So we see in the apostle Paul this principle of fatherhood clearly illustrated. He had begotten many sons in the faith and he expected them to honor him for that. We know that many of the churches didn't and subsequently got in trouble for rejecting the life and teaching they had received from their father. Nevertheless, he continue to appeal to them as their father hoping that they would come to their senses and recognize their need to honor him.

Perhaps the most important thing to glean from this is that a church's ability to fulfill its destiny and accomplish its purpose depends greatly on its willingness to honor its father. This was certainly true in the New Testament and it is true today as well. There is tremendous blessing released when a church honors its father. Unfortunately, as we shall see later in this book, many churches have not honored their father(s) with the result that they have exempted themselves from receiving great blessing. For the command to "honor your father and mother," while applying primarily to our immediate natural families, no doubt applies to spiritual fathers (and mothers) as well. We will explore this more fully in the next part of this book.

# Part 2

•

THE IMPORTANCE OF

# HONORING

## FATHERS

# 4

# BLESSINGS AND CURSES

In the first part of this book we have seen how important fathers are in the economy of God. God has called fathers to be those who share His own Father-heart and transmit it to others. It is through fathers that God initiates His work so that life is produced in many others. In the last days, God will especially use fathers to start many new and wonderful things He does in the earth. If we don't have fathers as role models, we will not raise up fathers to initiate the work. Only fathers can produce fathers.

In this second part of this book entitled Honoring Fathers, we will examine the attitude God desires his people to have towards those who are fathers. While we touched on this briefly we must now ex-plore it more fully. Much of the blessing that God has for his people depends on their attitude toward fathers. Just as there is a great promise attached to obeying earthly fathers and mothers ("that it may be well with you, and that you may live long on the earth,") so there is also great blessing attached to honoring spiritual fathers To ignore this is to cut ourselves off from much blessing that Father has in store for his church.

First, we must honor fathers simply because God Himself has honored them. The Word of God is full of statements of the honor that God expects fathers to receive. One of the things that we must settle right up front is that we don't honor fathers because they are perfect and have it all together. We must have no illusion about the fact that fathers are human and are not those who have reached a state of sinless perfection. We have seen this in the story of the fathers of the nation of Israel, Abraham, Isaac, and Jacob. Moses does not shield us from the reality of their lives but gives us a full account of them, warts and all! There was nothing special about these men apart from the operating grace of God working in their lives. God chose them and therefore He loved them. And because He loved them, He loved and chose their seed after them. That is why the New Testament says of their descendants:

"Concerning the gospel they are enemies for your sake, but concerning the election they are beloved for the sake of the fathers" (Romans 11:28)

This verse teaches us why it is so important to honor the fathers. Since it is through them that we have been given life we must honor them. The principle is clear: wherever life is involved there must be honor. And since all life runs all the way back to the Source, Our Creator Father, ultimate honor belongs to Him alone, the Source of all blessings and strength.

# Cursing Fathers

The book of Proverbs is full of statements about the proper relationship we must have towards our fathers. What many people don't understand is that Proverbs was a sort of discipleship manual for the nation of Israel. Since the goal for every Israelite was the development of a heart of wisdom, Proverbs provided practical instruction in gaining a wise and discerning heart. And right at the forefront of such wisdom was the proper treatment of parents as those who gave us life:

> "He who curses his father or his mother, his lamp will be put out in deep darkness" (Proverbs 20:20)

> "The eye that mocks his father and scorns obedience to his mother, the ravens of the valley will pick it out, and the young eagles will eat it." (Pro. 30:17)

Consulting Strong's Concordance for the meaning of the word curses in the above Scripture sheds some interesting light. It is defined as "to make light of, to make small or trifling; to abate; to bring into contempt or despise; to lightly esteem." Obviously, this differs from what we normally think of as cursing—chanting incantations over a boiling cauldron or some other thing associated with witchcraft. In fact, it does not even refer necessarily to speaking directly against your father, although it could certainly include that. Any form of lightly esteeming fathers or making light of them in the heart is a form of cursing them and brings God's judgment.

Thus, Proverbs says that the result of my making light in my heart of a father is that I will experience a lessening of light and understanding. If I don't repent the inevitable result may be the extinguishing of all light until I walk in total darkness. If this continues the result invariably is that I end up "walking in my own light" and this is disastrous. Witness what Isaiah says:

> "Look, all of you who kindle a fire, who encircle yourselves with sparks: walk in the light of your fire and in the sparks you have kindled—this you shall have from My hand: you shall lie down in torment." (Is 50:11) Emphasis mine.

It is necessary to have much light if we are going to build the church properly. If we lightly esteem fathers, it is a sure way to diminish or cut off the light from above. Judging from all the problems, failures, and lack of fruit in the churches, many seem to be walking in their own light.

A man can imitate the anointing of God for a time. Many are fooled by a persuasive personality, strong soul and natural giftings. To the undiscerning these can masquerade as the real anointing. So many projects and plans may seem good to the natural or intellectual mind and may even seem to succeed for a season. Yet nothing will produce lasting fruit unless it is initiated as light from Christ and maintained by the Holy Spirit. And only lasting fruit glorifies the Father.

## Spiritual Blindness and Pride

The light that comes from Christ casts no shadow. When we light our own fire we cannot help but cast a shadow. When we try to see by our own fire, there is always a shadow somewhere beyond us and our vision is impaired.

The quote from Proverbs 30:17 illustrates the same principle. Despising and mocking a parent will cause one to lose his eyesight. To be spiritually blind in these days is a most terrifying prospect for anyone who even slightly desires to lead God's people. Proverbs also speaks of another aspect of blindness:

> "There is a generation that curses its father, and does not bless its mother. There is a generation that is pure in its own eyes, yet is not washed from its filthiness" (Pro. 30:11-12).

This Scripture speaks of perhaps the most insidious form of spiritual blindness, pride. The writer speaks of a generation that is "pure in their own eyes", while, in reality, they are filthy before God. The result of pride is that they are deceived by it so that they cannot discover their real state before God.

Sadly, there are many leaders in the Body of Christ who are full of pride, yet remain blind to it. In leaders it often manifests in a refusal to work with others so that they become islands unto themselves. They feel no need for accountability or correction, in fact, they avoid it like the plague. They certainly don't understand God's plan to restore fathers and their need to be properly related to them. So they work alone and avoid any meaningful relationships, especially with those who are fathers. While they may excel in natural leadership and ability, accomplishing wonderful things for God, they themselves never submit to counsel from others. They will steadfastly avoid any personal relationships where they might be exposed.

In their defense, it must be said that many of these leaders have been turned off by so-called apostolic leaders who have not exhibited a true father's heart. The fleshly ambition seen in so many leaders today has left them with a bad taste in their mouth. Mention the word 'apostle' today and you can see apprehension appear on people's faces. Many have been hurt by legalism or by a hierarchical approach to apostolic leadership rather than a true, servant model. No wonder they find it difficult to trust those true fathers who could really do them good if they allowed themselves to be properly related to them.

This is why so many good leaders fall into sin. They are unable to see that they have not been "washed from the filthiness" in their own lives. There is no one to admonish them. Because of this and their refusal to be vulnerable in relationships with true fathers, they are missing out on the protection which God has provided in the Body. True fathers are intended by God to save their sons from much grief. How sad to see sons repeating the sins and mistakes of their fathers because they are too self-sufficient or proud to listen and accept counsel. Those who maintain an independent attitude pay for it in the long run.

At one time in his life, the apostle Peter was too proud and independent to accept what the Lord wanted to do in his life. On the eve of His Passion, when Jesus would wash the disciple's feet, Peter protested vehemently and resisted:

> "Peter said to Him, 'You shall never wash my feet!' Jesus answered him, If I do not wash you, you have no part with Me' (John 13:8).

Behind Peter's refusal was not a humble heart too unworthy to accept what Jesus wanted to do. Rather, it was a proud, independent heart that resisted! And the result was that Peter, at first, was unwilling to be washed by the Son of God. What a privilege he almost missed because of his pride and independence. Thankfully, the Lord worked patiently with his disciple until Peter was not only willing to have Jesus wash his feet, but his entire body as well.

What is important about this story is that Jesus extended this service to all of his people:

> "If I then, your Lord and Teacher, have washed your feet, you also ought to wash one another's feet" (John 13:14).

Contrary to popular opinion the Lord was not instituting the sacrament of foot washing at this point. What He was doing was defining the ministry of the body of Christ as the service of "washing one another" in Christ. We must overcome that independence which is natural to all and learn to both wash others as well as receive the washing. Refusal to do so can only be attributed to our pride and independence—"I don't need anybody to wash my feet."

This has particular relevance to the relationship between fathers and sons in these last days. Fathers will have to overcome ambition and a desire to control others and learn to wash the feet of their sons in true humility and love. This means that they will not be able to function in an independent spirit. Sons, on the other hand, must learn to receive the washing in an attitude of true honor and respect (which in turn will wash the heart of fathers). Do we see how God has so tempered this so that fathers need sons and sons need fathers?

John 1:12 states that only those who received Christ were able to become the sons of God. This of course is also true of fatherly counsel and input. Even Jesus apparently was not able, (or didn't choose) to do wonders where they didn't receive him (Matthew 3:58). Many times I have witnessed a tremendous impartation through a father just simply because he was received and honored as a father. It is amazing how the Holy Spirit can work supernaturally through a relationship when there is a receptive heart.

## A Story of Receiving

Recently I met with a younger man on the recommendation of another pastor, a spiritual son, with whom I had worked successfully for several years. This man was at the end of his rope and was thinking of leaving the ministry after twenty years of serving. He had spent the last several years building the church he was now pastoring. There were problems everywhere. He had worked himself into a real snit, angry with his elders and some of the people in the church. He was at the point of reacting negatively to any and all suggestions from the leaders of his church. He felt unappreciated for the hard work he had done over the years in bringing the church to its present state. He had indeed done much work, but relationships were shaky.

He started by saying that I had an excellent reputation in his eyes because of the testimony of two other brothers. Further, he implied that I was his last resort. He was ready to throw in the towel, but believed I could help him. As he talked and unfolded the story, I simply listened. Some of the things he was going through, I had experienced. I told him so. After about an hour of listening, I began to receive a couple of things to say to him from the Holy Spirit. They were not remedies for his woes, but more along the lines of understanding of where he was, and suggestions as to how to walk through the trials. I was able to gently rebuke him for his reactions to his leaders and others. He laughed and saw it instantly, and took the rebuke. Afterward he was deeply appreciative and seemed very encouraged. I felt like I had really said very little of great depth or substance to him, but apparently the Holy Spirit did something most important. He encouraged him. The key, however, was the younger man's openness to receive and the Holy Spirit used this to make me an instrument of encouragement.

We agreed to meet again, and to begin a regular dialogue. At some future point I knew we would get down to some nitty-gritty matters concerning doctrine, governmental matters and the like. He would receive, and this would open the door for his church leadership to receive. This could now happen because of the law of sowing and reaping. He is receiving, so they can now receive from him. Without his receptivity, none of this would have been possible. Also, without the good report concerning me from the other brethren, he would not have been set up to receive.

Many a young person in ministry has been helped by simple words of admonition and the encouragement of a father. The only requirement was that he was willing to receive. The Holy Spirit can move if we will open up and let him. A relationship, if genuine, is a vehicle for the Holy Spirit to manifest in. Many leave the ministry in discouragement  because they lack such a relationship. It was the salvation of Israel and Egypt as well, that Pharaoh listened to the wise counsel of Joseph, whom God had made a father to Pharaoh.

## Blessing: The Rechabite Principle

If dishonoring fathers brings a curse upon us the flip side is true—honoring them brings tremendous blessing!  In the last days, God will bless his people tremendously. One of the major ways He intends to do that is by raising up a generation of sons who will honor their fathers.

The Bible contains many wonderful statements regarding the blessing that flows to those who honor their fathers. But perhaps the best example in Scripture is that of the story of the Rechabites. Their story, found in Jeremiah chapter thirty-five, is a living example of how God blesses obedience. Yet it also provides us with great encouragement in the area of honoring fathers.

Jeremiah was instructed by God to place a test before the sons of one named Jonadab, the son of Rechab. The test was to place wine before them and ask them to drink with him. The Rechabites refused this invitation because their father had previously given them a command not to drink wine, neither they nor their sons forever. The Rechabites would not violate the command of their father and therefore refused Jeremiah remaining loyal to their pledge.

After the Rechabites refused the wine the word of God came to Jeremiah. He was to make a comparison between the loyalty of the sons of Rechab to their father and the disloyalty of the sons of Judah to their Father. If the Rechabites continued to honor the word their father had spoken to them, how much more should the children of Israel honor the word of the living God? But they did not and therefore were ripe for judgment.

What is amazing about the Rechabites is their absolute loyalty to their father; a loyalty that did not go unnoticed by God. God now speaks through Jeremiah that because of their obedience to their father the Rechabites would not "want a man to stand before Him forever" (Jer. 35:19). What an incredible promise! And all due to the fact that they honored their father's command and would not drink wine. Such honor was recorded by God and he blessed them beyond their wildest imagination.

This is a powerful story that demonstrates how blessing is attached to honoring fathers—both earthly fathers as well as spiritual. In these days of restoration when God is raising up fathers in the Body of Christ we must learn to honor them properly if we want God to bless us as He did with the Rechabites.

## A Good Attitude

What many people don't understand is that the same attitude of heart we have toward the heavenly Father is reflected by the attitude we have toward our earthly fathers. The writer of Hebrews seems to have understood this and makes it clear:

"Furthermore, we have had human fathers who corrected us, and we paid them respect. Shall we not much more readily be in subjection to the Father of spirits and live? For they indeed for a few days chastened us as seemed best to them, but He for our profit, that we may be partakers of His holiness" (Heb. 12:9-10, emphasis mine).

From God's comparison of the Rechabites with those who would not listen to the prophets, we may fairly draw the conclusion that dishonor or disobedience to an earthly father is a heart problem reflected by disobedience to God Himself. What the passage in Hebrews tells us is that disobedience brings a corresponding chastisement. Yet the flip side is equally true—obedience brings incredible blessing. And if we are obedient to God it will be manifest by our honoring those who are fathers in our midst.

In the next chapter we will explore this further by looking at the life of a man who excelled in this matter of honoring fathers. It is one of the reasons that David was designated by God as a "man after God's own heart."

# 5

# THE HEART OF
# DAVID

In the entire Word of God there is none who excels in the matter of having a right heart before God more than Israel's second king, David. He is God's benchmark of obedience and heart response for succeeding kings and leaders in Israel. In their obedience to God as well as their worship they were, for the most part, measured by the standard that their father David had set before them. Without doubt, David was one of the most blessed and successful leaders of all times.

There have been many attempts to understand the basis of David's success, yet it is not difficult to do. He seems to have learned early what God had told the prophet Samuel when he was chosen from his brothers, that "God looks at the heart and not the outward appearance." David knew God's heart and learned that blessing depended on his own heart attitude toward God and others. As evidence of that David also learned early the importance of honoring fathers if he was to live in blessing and receive revelation from God.

## David's Early History

We should start by recognizing that David, like many of us, did not have a perfect father who raised him. The Bible really doesn't say much about Jesse, David's earthly father and most of what we know about him is known primarily because of his relationship to his son. Yet we can read between the lines to understand a little of what David's early life was like.

After God had rejected Saul as king, the prophet Samuel was instructed to go to Bethlehem and anoint a king from the sons of Jesse (I Samuel16). He himself did not know which of Jesse's sons was God's choice. Yet he was told to invite Jesse and his sons to a sacrifice and there, God would identify which of his Jesse's sons he was to anoint.

At the feast Samuel reviewed each of Jesse's sons as they passed before him. Though each was impressive and Samuel was ready to anoint them, the Lord made it clear that He had rejected them. After all of the sons had passed before him Samuel inquired of Jesse, "Are all the young men here?" It was then that Jesse informed Samuel that there was one more son, David, who was tending the sheep and had not been invited to the feast. Samuel informed Jesse that they would not sit down to eat until David was brought in. When he arrived, God told Samuel to anoint him as the future king of Israel and Samuel obeyed.

What is amazing is that Jesse had not even thought David important enough to invite to the feast either because he was the youngest or for some other reason. It is not difficult to imagine that David must have felt some rejection at this point.

Apparently discord had been brewing in the family for some time, because, at a later date, David suffered even a greater rejection. When David's three brothers had gone to fight against Goliath with Saul's army, David was apparently at home for a season looking after his father's sheep. His father sent him to visit his brothers at the battle front to take some home delicacies to them and some cheese to their captain.

Upon arriving and delivering the provisions David saw the giant Goliath come and utter his threats against Israel. When David asked about the reward for killing Goliath his brothers began to ridicule and humiliate him in front of everyone.

> "Now Eliab his oldest brother heard when he spoke to the men; and Eliab's anger was aroused against David, and he said, 'Why did you come down here? And with whom have you left those few sheep in the wilderness? I know your pride and the insolence of your heart, for you have come down to see the battle.' And David said, 'What have I done now? Is there not a cause?' Then he turned from him toward another and said the same thing; and these people answered him as the first ones did(I Samuel 17:28-30).

This attitude of derision in David's brothers towards him at that time certainly did not occur over night, but was an extension of their previous feelings about him. David was certainly discounted by his brothers, just as his father had discounted him when Samuel came to pick a king. They unjustly accused him of pride, yet in the process their own pride was clearly manifested.

I have observed in families how many times the youngest child will be discounted by his or her older siblings. Often he or she will be "put in a box", so to speak, and never get out of it in the eyes of his elders. It is strange to note that it is often hard for those who know us intimately to perceive God working maturity and perfection in us. Rather do they judge us according to the past and reject us. We can not grow up in their eyes. It is tragic when this type of attitude operates in a family or a church, when those who are mature cannot release the babes to come further in God. It results in a rejection of the true worth of the person.

In the midst of it all there is no record of David ever having an improper heart attitude towards his father or brothers. He was a perfectly obedient son, taking cheese and raisins to his brothers at the battle front when he was told. And in the midst of his brothers' rejection at the front he refused to wallow in self-pity, letting it cast a pall over his life and ministry. Rather, he kept his mind and spirit clear, so he could accurately hear God and took the opportunity to kill Goliath and win a great victory for the Lord and Israel.

## David's Submission to Saul

After Samuel secretly anointed David as Israel's future king, he was adopted into Saul's household and called to serve the king. It wasn't long before another rejection came to test him. This time, it came from a spiritual father. David's obvious anointing in warfare and leadership brought down the wrath of an insecure Saul. Prompted by an evil spirit, Saul would spend many years persecuting David, actually attempting to take his life on several occasions. Though many today complain about their father's treatment of them, how many have had a powerful warrior-king like Saul hurl a javelin at them and attempt to pin them to the wall? (I Sam 19: 10). At least twice in David's life he endured such treatment.

On at least two occasions, David had opportunity to kill Saul but refused, though his men urged him. On one of these occasions, (I Samuel 24:3-20) there is a beautiful story which demonstrates David's heart towards Saul. In tender terms, David refers to Saul as "his father" (vs. 11), while Saul refers to him as "his son" (vs. 16). So tender was David's heart towards his father that he was smitten in conscience for even cutting off Saul's robe. The robe of the king represented his station (reputation) in life and David was broken for violating that reputation in any way, even the cutting off of a small piece. Would to God that the Body of Christ was as sensitive in treating fellow members! How often, while avoiding an overt attack of others we will still insinuate something about a person in order to undermine his or her position. David refused to do that. He would allow no root of bitterness to spring up in his heart, even though he was being rejected. Regardless of Saul's behavior he was a father and David behaved himself properly towards him before God. It is interesting to note that David's reward for his behavior was to receive a prophetic statement from Saul himself that he would not only prosper, but would himself be king one day (v. 20).

## How Sweet It Is

Twice in my life I received wonderful, encouraging prophecy from someone who was in severe opposition to me. My favorite memory of this comes from the day I was ordained back about thirty years ago. A truly prophetic but undisciplined man who had continually caused havoc in the church, popped in half way through the meeting and took a seat in the back of the hall. I had just solidly rebuked him several days before for certain behavior and asked him to refrain from prophesying for a season. He had left very upset with me stating that he would not be back. And there he was. I elected to try to refrain from making any show of discontent at that time, and prayed silently that God would not let him open his mouth, for I felt he meant me no good. Suddenly he stood up and in a booming voice began one of the most encouraging prophecies concerning my future that I ever was privileged to receive . Part of his prophecy was to the effect of Is 54:17, that no weapon formed against me would ever prosper. That prophecy has meant much over the years as various battles have raged. I knew that that prophecy had to be from God, for I am sure that he would not have originated it in his own heart. I have fought a good warfare sustained by that prophecy on many occasions.

I can only imagine that David hung onto the prophecy delivered by Saul in 1 Sam 24:20. I can see in my mind's eye, David huddled in his cloak on many a dark night, reviewing and savoring that word from God in his heart.

## David Honors Saul

Refusing to take matters in his own hands, God honored David and finally delivered him from Saul. In this, David shines even more than when Saul was alive. Who would have blamed David for rejoicing at the news of Saul's death and gloating in his victory? Yet David continued to honor Saul as he did when he was alive. You see, it was in David's heart to honor a father on principle, not because of his perceived worthiness, nor for political reasons.

When Saul had died on the mountains of Gilboa, it was the men of Jabesh-Gilead that retrieved Saul's and Jonathan's bodies from the wall at Bethshan and gave them a proper burial. This was in response to the fact that Saul had rallied Israel's army and defended the men of Jabesh-Gilead when they were being attacked.[1] One of the first acts of David after becoming king was to commend the men of Jabesh-Gilead for honoring Saul. David would have been justified in trying to wipe out the memory of Saul and consolidate his own position for Abner, Saul's former commander, was already attempting to garner support to overthrow David and retain the kingdom. Yet David understood the principle of honoring a father, even though he had been so badly mistreated by him during his life. In New Testament terms he knew the truth of giving "honor to whom honor was due" (Romans 13:7). This was a fundamental principle of life to him and one that would bring him life and prosperity.

Upon Saul's death, David publicly lamented with fasting and weeping over Saul (2 Samuel 1). He also had Saul's Amalekite slayer put to death in a display of genuine grief and horror at the young man's lack of respect for God's anointed. David then sent for Saul's bones and brought them up to be buried with great honor in the family sepulcher of Kish, Saul's father. David kept on honoring Saul for many years after his death. He knew the commandment to "honor your father and mother" and received the blessing that accompanies it.

## Honoring Fathers Today

The example of David is a powerful incentive for young men today. There are many who have been temporarily placed in situations where they are subjected to men like Saul, who do not have their best interests at heart. Some of them are even being severely mistreated and asked to submit to horrendous situations. We have heard the horror stories over the years of how those in authority have spiritually abused those under them in the name of submission.

While such abuse is never justified, God often uses such situations to teach young men and women how to honor fathers regardless of their treatment of them. We must settle this principle in our hearts that to "honor fathers is to honor God." When we find ourselves in such circumstances our precious God has not abandoned us, but has much to teach us out of his great heart. As always the question is not "have we been wronged," but "how are we choosing to respond?" Will we honor even those who abuse us because we have learned the deep lesson that God honors fathers?

Unfortunately, there are many who fail this test and despise those fathers in their life. They are embittered and can say nothing good about them. They can only talk about the abuse or neglect they suffered at their hands and therefore give them no honor. How easily David could have succumbed to that spirit and ended up despising and dishonoring Saul. We are sure that he could have found many in Israel that would have commiserated with his bitterness. Yet the "man after God's own heart" rose above it and honored Saul long after Saul was gone and he had inherited the throne. He knew the truth that God honors fathers and practiced it in his own life.

Of course, at the heart of David's willingness to honor Saul was a healthy fear of God. It is unlikely that we will give honor to fathers, especially those who abuse us, if we do not have that respect for God that transforms all human relationships. This is what made David the "man after God's own heart." And it is that alone that will allow us to give proper honor to those whom God has put in our life, even if they have not acted with our best interest at heart. May God raise up a generation of men and women in this hour who, like David, can be said to be men and women after God's own heart.

1 This is a wonderful story which indicates the immeasurable value of the vertical relationship which can bring deliverance in a time of need. The men of

Jabesh were in dire straits and asked the newly appointed King to help them. The story is found in 1 Samuel 11:1-11 and should be read thoroughly at this point

# Part 3

•

## THE PROPER FUNCTION OF

# FATHERS

# 6

# HONORING SONS AND DAUGHTERS

We have seen in the previous chapter that God expects sons and daughters to give proper honor to natural and spiritual fathers. Not only is this a clearly stated principle of God's word, it is intended to be the means of great blessing in our lives. Life, blessing, revelation, and prosperity all flow from such obedience. To their credit there have been many young men who have behaved properly towards spiritual fathers and have been greatly blessed in the process.

We have also seen that God expects this honor towards fathers, even if the fathers are not deserving of it. David is a powerful example of a man who honored a spiritual father in his life who certainly was not worthy. God blessed him for it and David was given the authority that had previously been Saul's.

That being said, how much better it would be if, unlike Saul, fathers behaved in such a way that the sons would have no difficulty honoring and submitting to them. In this part of this book we want to look at the problem of many would be fathers: Making it difficult for sons and daughters to relate properly. In this, and in later parts of the book we will look at those godly heart traits that would alleviate the strain and push forward the Lord's kingdom. What we must see is that as fathers embody these traits in their lives they make it easy for sons to honor them and blessings flow automatically from above. Conversely, if some of these things I speak of exist in a leader's life, then we will always see turmoil, hurt and lack of life and anointing. It is not God's best for sons and daughters to have to honor or submit to fathers in spite of how they act but rather because of it. Fathers are those who are to excel in certain traits so that they are afforded honor by all those around them.

## Saulish Leaders

One of the problems among leaders in the Body of Christ today is that many of them have mistakenly drawn their concept of leaders and how they function from the world. The world's concept of leaders is that they sit on the top of the heap, having all of the authority. They make the fatal mistake of equating leadership with position and authority.

We have seen in the previous chapter that this was the concept of leadership that Saul had. Since he had neither fear of or faith in God, he believed he had to maintain his authority from whoever assaulted it, real or perceived. He had forgotten that it was God who had given him his position and authority in Israel. Having lost vital connection to God, he embarked on a crusade to protect his throne from any would-be usurper. This led, of course, to deception and the paranoia which usually follows. Wrongly assuming that David was trying to take his throne, he spent the remaining years of his kingdom trying to kill one of his most trusted servants who had demonstrated nothing but perfect loyalty.

Unfortunately, there are many Saulish leaders in the Church today. Having no vital relationship to God, they live their lives in the apprehension that someone might steal their ministry or take their authority. This usually has devastating results if that man is a pastor of a church. Often, a Saulish pastor will resort to manipulation and other soulish tactics to get people to do what he wants to do. It is all justified in the name of "saving the church" or "protecting the sheep," but it really has to do with a man "protecting his turf." This often has devastating results leaving in its path those whose lives are wrecked by leaders who began with a genuine desire to minister to others and end up playing God instead.

The results are even more hurtful in the case of apostles who have authority or influence over many churches. I have personally witnessed the abuse that has occurred when men claiming apostolic authority have sought to direct the affairs of local churches with little or no regard for local leadership. Wielding apostolic authority can be heady stuff and when those yielding it take their cue from Saul the result is often devastated lives and a weakening of the root of real authority.

What is the problem with such leaders? The problem is not with the notion that such men should have authority—it is that such authority is being wielded by those who lack the essential understanding, maturity and character traits for leadership in the Body of Christ. For the truth is, anointed leaders in the Body of Christ are those who exercise authority properly through a Christ-like character and through a relationship with those whom they govern. True apostles are those with real authority delegated to them from Jesus Christ Himself! The notion that only authority is involved in oversight, without deep and meaningful relationships, is ludicrous and has led to the lack of flow and anointing we have seen in a lot of groups.

This must be understood if we are going to see true fathers emerge on the scene today. For fathers must be those who speak and act with authority, yet without being authoritative. Such men can exercise real authority because in their character they exhibit the nature of the Lamb. And like the Lamb they must demonstrate the "meekness and gentleness" which are in Christ.

## Meekness and Gentleness

Ask most people today what are the most important characteristics of true leadership and you will rarely find meekness and gentleness at the top of the list. Yet as we have seen, God's idea of the most important qualifications for leaders and ours are often very different. That becomes even more apparent when we realize how God views this all-important trait of meekness and gentleness. In the world, this quality is never associated with leadership. Yet in the kingdom it is an indispensable quality for those who would lead men, especially those who are fathers in the faith.

We can look at both the Old and New Testaments to find numerous examples of this quality in God's people. We have already seen how David is a role model for how sons should relate to fathers. David is further an excellent role model of a leader. David himself excelled in this quality of meekness and gentleness as a leader. How did he learn the importance of this quality? It seems that he first learned it by seeing that it was the way in which God Himself had dealt with him:

"You have also given me the shield of Your salvation; your right hand has held me up, your gentleness has made me great. You enlarged my path under me; so my feet did not slip. I have pursued my enemies and overtaken them; neither did I turn back again till they were destroyed. I have wounded them, so that they could not rise; they have fallen under my feet"(Psalm 18:35-38).

In this passage, David acknowledges that his heavenly Father had made him great even in the violent pursuit of warfare. This scripture makes it clear that the molding factor in his success was gentleness—God's gentleness had a deep effect on him. David uses the word anvah for gentleness, a Hebrew word that simply means humility or meekness. What a statement! David said that it was God's very humility, his 'stooping down' to help him that made him successful in what he did. This should lay to rest forever the notion that gentleness is to be associated with weak leadership. Since it is the way that God deals with people we should never think of it as being out of fashion.

## Lovingkindness is Better than Life.

Once there was a man who had a teenage son who was exactly like him in his temperament. Both father and son were strong type "A" personalities, and they were doers and achievers. They loved each other very much, but inevitable clashes began to come as the boy sought to establish his own identity and emerge into man-hood.

The father had pushed very hard for many years in building his "empire," and in doing so, had not really done what he should have toward securing the relationship with his son. He had neglected this important matter. This, coupled with the natural insensitivity of his personality type, caused a growing problem. A push on the part of the son to establish his own ground developed slowly into a rebellious attitude, since the father didn't take kindly to the slightest opposition. He wasn't used to "subordinates" speaking up to him. This son, cut out of the same mold, stood up more and more. One day he stood eyeball to eyeball (in fact slightly taller than his father) and refused to obey a direct order. In a flash of revelation, the father suddenly realized that he was powerless to do anything about this immediate situation, short of a fistfight. He wasn't so sure he could even win that. Ten years earlier he would have taken off his belt, and the whole thing would have been resolved.

He turned and slowly walked away, with a hollow feeling that he had just lost some authority. He began to talk seriously with the Lord about this son. Instead of receiving a new revelation on how to lead, he was surprised to hear the Lord say, "Loving kindness is better than life, just love him instead of commanding him and see what happens."

The father loved this son very deeply and was truly disturbed by the turn of events. He began to totally reverse his tactics. There would be no more authoritative manner, but love and acceptance. Fishing trips with genuine fellowship ensued. There was an attempt to treat the son with respect, as though he were an adult.

A few months later, in January, the two were on a deep sea fishing trip in the Florida Keys. The father had been sick for some time, but was recuperating. Suddenly the temperature began to drop. The place they were staying had no heat. About three o'clock in the morning, the father was dimly aware that someone was hovering over his bed in the  dark. It was the son who had gotten up, gone to the car parked about a block away, obtained a car robe, and was now placing it gently over the father. Realizing he had wakened the older man, the son said, "I love you, Dad. I didn't want you to get cold." The father's heart was warmed more than his body.

As time went by, the father discovered that his real authority had never diminished but in fact had grown. The son readily came to him for counsel. A tremendous relationship developed which allowed the father to truly "cover" his son while he was achieving manhood and his own sense of wholesome independence. Gentleness truly makes one great and loving kindness is far better than life.

When we come to the New Testament none excels in this quality more than the great apostle to the Gentiles, Paul. People often erroneously perceive Paul to have been a very obstinate man with whom it was difficult to get along. It is true that he was a man of great resolve who would not be deterred from accomplishing his mission. Yet that does not mean that he was difficult in his dealings with God's people. The truth is, he was the very epitome of gentleness when dealing with those who were called in Christ as he himself reminded the Thessalonians:

> "But we were gentle among you, just as a nursing mother cherishes her own children. So, affectionately longing for you, we were well-pleased to impart to you not only the gospel of God, but also our own lives, because you had become dear to us." (I Thessalonians 2:7-8)

How rarely we think of Paul in this manner. It is true that Paul was a man of great faith and courage, yet he regards himself as a nursemaid towards his own spiritual children. For Paul, this is one of the main evidences of his apostolic credentials. Gentleness is, after all, a fruit of the Holy Spirit.

Sadly, this quality is often lacking in those considered apostolic leaders today. Numerous examples could be cited demonstrating how many in apostolic oversight today lack this quality. We have seen apostolic leaders, unable to resolve church problems quickly, sell off buildings, fire pastors without scriptural or ethical reasons and put their own people in place. They make pronouncements and decisions without fully investigating and knowing the mind of the Lord. Sadly, due to their lack of gentleness and patience, such men have left many devastated lives in their wake and many potential leaders are shipwreck because of them.

It is obvious that both David and Paul reflected the leadership model of Jesus in their own lives. Paul seems to have understood this when addressing the Corinthians:

> "Now I Paul, myself am pleading with you by the meekness and gentleness of Christ—who in presence am lowly among you, but being absent am bold toward you"(II Cor. 10:1)

Even Jesus during His earthly life spoke of this quality as that which would appeal to his hearers and bid them to come (Matthew 11:28-29). The importance of this quality cannot be underestimated, especially since the Lord cites it as his chief characteristic inducing men to follow Him. And once we realize how important it is that this quality be seen in our lives, all the more in those who are fathers, the more effective we will become. It may not be over-emphasizing it to say that fathers above all else, must be those who excel in gentleness and meekness.

## The Grace of Being Teachable

While it is easy to cite numerous texts asserting the importance of this quality it is not as easy to define it. Yet if there is one word above all that practically expresses what is at the heart of gentleness and meekness it would have to be the word teachable. When we have learned meekness and gentleness it will be obvious in our willingness to receive from others. This is even more important for leaders, especially those who would be fathers in the faith.

This goes to the heart of our concept of leadership. Far too many leaders have the idea that real leadership is the ability to boss others around and remain at the top of the pecking order. They certainly will not receive from those they consider to be underlings. It all comes down to the fact that they have embraced a worldly concept of leadership, one that Jesus acknowledged as typifying the Gentiles of his day (Matthew 10:25-26). That was not to characterize those of His kingdom! Rather than being perceived as those at the top, He insisted that true leaders in the kingdom consider themselves at the bottom of the heap—the ones who get to serve everyone else!

This grace to be teachable is critical to the success of any leader, and especially that of fathers. It is not an exaggeration to say that Moses, as great a leader as he was, would not have made it if it wasn't for the fact that he could receive correction from his father-in-law who wisely discerned that he was counseling too much (Exodus 17:13-27). How is it that the man who met God face to face on the mount could not see that he was taxing both himself and the people by his actions? The simple answer is that even the best leaders have blind spots—those areas where they are unable to see themselves as others do. While God may choose to speak to them directly, he often will use others to point them out. If we cannot receive from others then we are putting ourselves in the place of refusing help from God. To Moses' credit he was not only teachable, he could receive, of all people, from his father-in-law. That is perhaps one of the greatest miracles of his ministry. This is part of the reason why the Holy Spirit says that he was the meekest man upon the earth (Num. 12:3).

It is critical that fathers exhibit this quality in their lives. They must be willing to receive from others and that means even a rebuke when necessary. In this regard, the Scripture again seems to present David as a perfect example of this trait. When Nathan the prophet rebuked him for his adultery and murder (II Samuel 11), David received the rebuke and deeply humbled himself before the

Lord. Later, David would write these great words found in Psalm 25:4-5,9):

> "Show me Your ways, O Lord; teach me Your paths. Lead me in
> your truth and teach me, for You are the God of my salvation; on You
> I wait all the day. The humble He guides in justice, and the humble
> He teaches His way"(emphasis mine)

Another Old Testament example of the importance of being teachable is found in the story of the healing of Naaman in Second Kings, chapter five. Namaan, captain of the Syrian army, was a leper. A small Jewish maiden who was a servant to Naaman's wife told her about the prophet in Samaria who could cure her husband of his leprosy. With permission from the king, Naaman went to the prophet Elisha who told him what was required for his healing. He was to wash himself "seven times in the Jordan River" if he was to be healed (5:10). Yet upon hearing this Naaman was offended. For one, the prophet himself never even came out to see him but rather, sent a servant to deliver the message. Besides, Naaman was instructed to wash himself in the Jordan, an ignoble river compared to the rivers of Syria as far as he was concerned. With his pride wounded, Naaman turned away in a rage and rejected the instructions of the prophet.

Thankfully, another servant of Naaman's reasoned with him and Naaman reluctantly obeyed the prophet's word and was healed. The result was not only the restoration of his flesh, but a revelation that the God of Israel was the true and living God whom He would now worship (5:15-19).

Twice the Lord used subordinates to speak the truth to this extremely powerful and proud man. In his pride, Naaman could not see that God was speaking to him through those he considered insignificant. When we are proud and unteachable we often miss those times when God is speaking to us. God may (and very often does) have something to say through the very least of the brethren if we are able to hear it. The problem is, we often fall into a subtle elitism in which we refuse to humble ourselves and listen to others, especially those whom we consider subordinate. This is often a problem for leaders who are unwilling to listen to those deemed lesser and only receive from those they consider to be peers. This can carry over into relationships between children and parents as well. Teenagers often feel that their parents don't really listen to them, especially their fathers, and that the fathers treat them as less important than themselves. While teenagers definitely should be subordinate to their parents, how blessed it is when fathers make their children feel like they have something worthwhile to say and want to listen!

## Honoring the Sons

Since God can speak at any time through anyone He chooses it is extremely important to esteem those around us by being teachable. This sets the stage for them to come and help us. Perhaps the apostle Paul summed it up best when he told the church at Rome:

> "Who are you to judge another man's servant? To his own master he stands or falls. Indeed, he will be made to stand, for God is able to make him stand."(Romans 14:4)

Everyone who is born again and is baptized into the Body of Christ is technically a servant of Christ and has immeasurable worth and value. Therefore, when we demean anyone in the church in our heart we are offending the Lord, who is both their

Master and ours. And those we demean, especially the younger person or peer, can always sense when they are not being honored or esteemed.

Fathers must be those who esteem and honor their sons, thus making it easier for them to receive. This is the spirit that the apostle Paul seems to have moved in when he was among the churches he founded. While he makes it clear that he could have come and exercised his authority as an apostle, he chose rather to come in a humble spirit honoring those he moved among. And this is the spirit that true fathers must walk in if they want to impart to sons in the faith.

Unfortunately, there is often a spirit of elitism today among those claiming to be apostles which is the very antithesis of the manner Paul walked. It manifests itself in an attitude which says: "I am an apostle and therefore I know more than you. Because of my anointing, I am somewhat infallible. Sit down and let me tell you what you need to know." While few would ever give voice to such a thing in public it often exists in their hearts and controls their actions. The result is that it places higher value on "position" than on relationship.

Several times in my life I have been involved in oversight situations in local churches where there has been a struggle for control. As such I have had to deal with men from outside who were trying to affect the local situation. They were trying to get in "through a side door" or "over a wall" as it were, and had no real regard for the leadership which was in place. Often they were simply trying to usurp authority (which we will speak later). They believed that their perceived position in the Kingdom was such that it gave them the right to overstep local authority and thus had little regard for my role as overseer or the other leadership. What impression do young sons get when they see fathers disregarding authority? The results are always that it breeds confusion and usually leaves many hurting people in its wake. It also raises up sons who in their own time have little regard for authority.

Many times when there are troubles in a church, there is a rebellious faction of people involved. Rebellion almost always feeds on some kind of perceived authority, even if it is spurious. The enemy will always see to it that the rebellious ones gravitate to any outside perceived authority which is questioning the local established authority. The times I have witnessed this I am convinced that the invaders meant no real harm. Their ambition and desire for greater territory was simply leading them to try to move landmarks denoting authority. They imagined that their calling and position put them somehow above lines of relationship. That is always a pathway to trouble and further confusion.

Such an attitude sets men and women at naught, especially the younger and lesser. Yet such a way is not the way of a true father in the kingdom. Paul was Timothy's father in the faith, but he demonstrated none of this elitism in his heart. He exhorted all of the churches to fully receive his young son and commanded them to respect him and not despise his youth. Paul considered himself as the "least of the apostles." This is remarkable! As the least he did not need to continually protect his reputation or make sure that all of the churches looked only to him, but could push them towards Timothy. This is one of the main attributes of an apostle; to be able to see the treasure hidden in the earthen vessels of sons who are possibly team members.

Elitism tends to make one overlook the potential God has placed in others. It looks for whatever can serve and elevate itself, rather than what will serve and elevate the Kingdom of Christ. It will discount the gifts and anointing God has placed in the Body. It is not teachable and is usually very critical of others. Scripture is clear that God hates this attitude (Proverbs 6:16-17), this haughty spirit and proud look which so easily discounts others.

We have so little time left! The church is generally suffering from a lack of forward impetus and enthusiasm. Certainly one of the remedies is to convince our sons and daughters of their value and worth in the scheme of God's plan and release them to it. Yet this can only occur when there are fathers who can nurture them, giving them the honor they are due as vessels the Holy Spirit can use. Only then will they have the confidence both in God and themselves to do all the will of God. Only then can they be effectively released into the grand ministries awaiting them in these end times.

# 7

# MACHO MEN AND ROLE MODELS

What happens when the television camera pans the sidelines at a football game? As the athletes realize they are on TV they wave wildly, grin broadly and shout, "Hey, Mom!" In all the games I have ever watched, I have yet to see one player, when the camera focuses on him, yell "Hey, Dad!" While occasionally an athlete with a good relationship with his father will say something about him in an interview, it is still rare. Most young men instinctively speak of their mothers rather than their fathers in those situations. Apparently there are not many good father-son relationships among sports figures and presumably among young men in general.

Many young men today enter marriage and sire babies with no earthly clue as to what fatherhood means (that is if they marry at all). Many young men create babies with no intention of marrying and taking responsibility. That's because most young in our culture have not had good role models of a father. They have been nurtured by Hollywood and TV stereotypes, having grown up with shows like The Brady Bunch or the Bill Cosby Show. These shows portray fathers as bumbling idiots saved only by the efforts of a super capable wife or super children whose genes must have come from an earlier generation.

In the last forty years, the Women's Liberation Movement and other women's groups have had a major influence on the way we now think about men in our culture. These groups have succeeded in dismissing the idea of the husband as the protective covering for his wife and in downgrading the importance of fatherhood. Many women today have completely dismissed the role of father. Producing children through in- vitro fertilization, the resulting children may never be properly influenced by a male father figure for the whole of their lives. We are just now coming to grips with the implications of this for our society and it is devastating! While sociologists and government officials like to blame various other sources for society's ills, they rarely if ever mention the breakdown of the family and the absence of real fathers as the real reason for much of society's problems.

The growth of industry and education has put more men into careers taking them increasingly away from home. Success is largely determined today in business or economic terms and many men will do just about anything to achieve it. Athletes are paid million dollar contracts for their athletic prowess. Unfortunately, such success is often accompanied with a laxness of morals. Who has not seen the multi-million dollar athlete with the fast car and the gorgeous women hanging all over him? And what is sad is that many athletes as well as movie stars and politicians placed high on the ladder of success are young people not at all ready for such success. As the young in our society observe them they get the message that this is what is meant by success. How many young people in our culture view being a successful father as their primary definition of success in life? Not many!

The Devil wants to destroy the godly image of fatherhood, which is what Jesus came to portray and restore. Along with this distorted picture of manhood is the notion that real manhood is determined by the number of "sexual conquests" one can make. Far too many women have been willing to accommodate this distorted view of manhood. No wonder sex is so cheapened in our society. For many today, adultery and fornication are not even equated with sin. Today, most young people have the idea that it is not whether to have sex or not, but what kind of protection to use that matters.

## Distorted Views of Success in the Church

It would be sad enough if this distortion of the meaning of success was limited only to our secular culture. Sadly, it has crept into the church as well. We can see it in the fact that many leaders, instead of concerning themselves with nurturing younger men and women, are busy constructing their ministries or futures. Why are many leaders engaged in this and ignoring the obvious? One of the reasons is that the church often measures success in the same way that the world does—by doing instead of being. Like many typical fathers who go off to work each day and come home too tired to be a father and husband, these leaders have a perverted view of success. The result is that very often they spend their time doing things that others can see and that are deemed important to achieving success, and not doing the things that really make a leader successful.

Real fathers are desperately needed if the situation is to change. They will prepare the children adequately for the future insuring that they will not squander what is given to them. We have all seen in the natural how one generation will build an empire and then when the time comes to hand it over, the next generation will struggle to maintain it. Very often this is a result of the fact that the children were never mentored in practical things and thus could not maintain the successes of the previous generation.

The real challenge for fathers in our day is to properly mentor sons so that they understand what real success is in the kingdom of God. Yet before fathers can do this they themselves must understand it and live in its reality. Far too many of those called to be fathers have been caught up in kingdom building, more concerned with their own futures than those of their sons. Fathers must step up to the plate and be counted. They must move away from mere busy work and prepare a generation for their God-given destiny.

## A Distorted View of Manhood

I can vividly remember when the oldest of my four sons was born. My father was a medical doctor and the birth took place in the hospital where he maintained his practice in Pathology. When the baby was born he came by shortly afterwards keenly interested in the health of his new grandson. He provided us with insight into what had just happened from a medical standpoint. He was very proud of his new grandson and of me, his son. Yet ethical and philosophical thoughts about fathering and the future that lay before us were never discussed. That was not surprising though, since he had never offered any in the past, nor were they ever discussed in the years following. He taught me many wonderful things but they all lay in the academic realm. He drilled me in mathematics when I was young and gave me a love for learning and science. One of our favorite pastimes was discussing Sherlock Holmes and improving our powers of observation.

Our family history can be traced back to the hills of North Alabama. My father, one of several brothers, singlehandedly put himself through college, medical school, internship, and a residency in pathology in two of the finest medical programs in the north. He was the only one of his siblings to get a higher education. While in medical school he was teased about his southern speech but by determined study, became an expert in the proper use of the English language. He loved the dictionary, and growing up we had a foot thick Funk and Wagnall's dictionary in our home. Eventually, dad became a founding fellow of the College of American Pathology. He had papers published in English and American journals of medicine. At the end of World War II, then a Lieutenant Commander in the Navy, he was selected to head the United States Naval medical team that went into Nagasaki and Hiroshima after the two atomic bombs were dropped to investigate the effects on the civilians. I was very proud of him.

However, when my father and grandfather were growing up in Alabama, gunfights and whiskey were considered the tokens of real manhood. Therefore, my father thought I should learn to handle alcohol at an early age and at about eight years of age he introduced me to hard liquor. Though he did not urge me to drink, he viewed it as a teaching experiment—part of my "manly" education to prepare me for the future. I do not fault my father for this. I know that he meant well. I wonder how many men are taught, directly or indirectly, by wrong example how to be men. Where I went to college in the south, many young men grew up thinking that manliness consisted of sports, alcohol, hunting, fishing, and girl chasing. This was not just typical of the south. I had spent my elementary school and teen years in Massachusetts and I noticed no difference in the way young men behaved there. Just as in the south, there men seemed to confuse "macho" with "manhood." I am sure that I am not the only one who had much baggage to be stripped of upon coming to Christ.

Being in control is another aspect of the male side of things that I was subtly taught. To be in charge and command others is always a desirable thing to the natural man. The independence of the American male spirit is established at an early age. The entrepreneurial spirit, as practiced in America finds fertile soil for its roots in the flesh, and we understand that the flesh contains nutrients of idolatry, sorcery, contentions, dissensions and selfish ambition (Gal 5:20). Self will is to be expressed. Witchcraft, which is sorcery, is nothing but an attempt to control others and one's own destiny! At my high school graduation, William E. Henley's poem, Invictus , was read, "I am the master of my fate, I am the captain of my soul."

This cultural and fleshly baggage comes into the church even if we are not aware of it. If we are ever to raise up young men as role models of true fatherhood, the counterfeit attitudes of false manhood and fatherhood must go. Because of the aforementioned personal role models and associations of youth, the Lord had to put me on a rough and difficult trail of renovation. I had plenty of zeal and a genuine love for the Lord. But mixed in there was an entrepreneurial spirit coupled with ambition, a false idea of success, plus a desire for recognition. The Lord had to crush this. I had to be rejected to learn the importance of not rejecting others. Rather, I was taught how to properly esteem them. There were times when I really and truly wondered if the Holy Spirit was not my worst enemy.

As I progressed on this path, however, certain marvelous blessings began to occur. These bolstered my spirit and let me know that Christ was changing me. Young men would come to me along the path and indicate that they looked at me as father in the Lord. As this occurred more and more often, I cried out to the Lord. How could I be a father figure to anyone? I didn't consider myself that way, and had plenty of past failure to prove it. I can remember talking to the Lord about this problem one day. He very clearly told me to quit thinking negatively. He said that He was making me into a father. Then He directed me to a scripture in Genesis 45:8.

> "So it was not you who sent me here, but God; and He has made me a father to Pharaoh, and Lord of all his house, and a ruler throughout all the land of Egypt."

The good news is that God is able to make the worst of us fathers! He wants to raise and release fathers in these last days. He is still teaching sinners in the way (Ps 25:8). I am so grateful for His patience, longsuffering and loving kindness.

The trip from "macho" man to godly father is painful, but worth every step. Much is at stake. Let's get on the path with all speed possible.

# 8

# Devilish ambition

History books as well as the Holy Bible reveal that much killing has occurred as a result of ambition. Upon coming to the throne, young kings have murdered their siblings to consolidate their positions. Sons have killed fathers. There is something wrong in the hearts of many men that causes jealousy to arise when a sense of competition sets in.

There is a well known fable that illustrates this in Ralph G. Turnbull's classic book, A Minister's Obstacles:

> "As the account goes, the devil was crossing the Libyan desert when he came upon a group of lesser fiends who were tempting a holy hermit. They tried him with seductions of the flesh; they sought to sour his mind with doubts am and fears; they told him that all his austerities

were worth nothing. But is was of no avail; the holy man was impeccable. Then the devil stepped forward. Addressing the imps, he said, 'Your methods are too crude. Permit me for one moment. This is what I should recommend'. Going up to the hermit, he said, ' Have you heard the news? Your brother has been made the Bishop of Alexandria'. The fable says that a scowl of jealousy began to cloud the serene face of the holy man" (A Minister's Obstacles, page 37, Ralph G. Turnbull, Baker Book House, 1964).

While this story amply illustrates the devilish effects of carnal ambition it needs to be said that not all ambition is of the demonic or fleshly kind. In fact, Scripture commends a certain type of ambition that might well be called "kingdom ambition." For instance, the apostle Paul makes it clear that having a desire to be a bishop (overseer) in the church is a good and worthy ambition (I Timothy 3:1). In fact, such a desire is a prerequisite to holding the office and must be evident if the person is to be considered. Apparently, ambition for the advancement of Christ's kingdom is never wrong but is a good thing. We need to clearly separate kingdom ambition from self-ambition.

The question that must always be asked is, "Where is our ambition aimed? Is it for Christ and His kingdom or is it for our own personal advancement?" Human or self-ambition is clearly Satanic in origin having its roots in Satan's own self-promotion. It is traditionally believed that it is Satan speaking in the fourteenth chapter of Isaiah promoting himself above the very throne of God. (14:13-14) This self-aggrandizement has at its core the desire to have the attention and worship due only to God. And it was this ambition that apparently turned a beautiful seraph into the prince of evil, the sworn enemy of God and his purpose in the universe.

Contrast Satan's great self-declarations in Isaiah with Jesus' own declaration of His Person in the Gospel of John. Seven times He cites the Old Testament divine designation I Am in reference to Himself. Yet this is not self-ambition, but the truthful declaration of a Man whose identity was totally rooted in God. Jesus had no interest in His own exaltation nor did He care what men thought about Him. His security was totally in His Father who willed the exaltation of the Son. Exaltation of self always has its roots in the evil one.

In this chapter, we want to expose devilish ambition for what it is. This is critical in regards to those who would be fathers. Real fathers must be those who, like the Lord Jesus, have no ambition except to see Christ exalted and His Kingdom extended.

## Wrong Ambition

It is true that God constructed us so we would desire the love and friendship of others. It is only when that desire for approval is placed above the approval of God that what is good becomes perverted and sinful. And it is a sad fact that many leaders today seem to find their own identity by seeking the approval of others. This, in turn, often leads to wrong ambition and some men have built their entire ministries on such ambition.

It is not difficult to detect wrong ambition, especially in leaders since it is easily detected in the actions that it inspires. It has a smell of its own. It is often accompanied by a controlling spirit which Scripture states is akin to witchcraft. Before witchcraft becomes demonic it is first a work of the flesh as the apostle Paul makes abundantly clear (Galatians 5:20). Those moving in ambition only look to manipulate people and use them for their own purpose and end. They look to take authority when they can get away with it and are unable to submit to others. They are not team players. It is also manifest in a tendency to constantly put down other people and their ideas if they feel in the least bit threatened. It puts others in boxes, categorizes them, and files them away, never to rise above a certain level in the eyes of the leader. The sad thing is, those leaders moving in ambition usually view people as stepping stones, only having worth in regards to their own plans.

There is a passage in 1 Samuel 14:52 that gives us a small glimpse into ambition as it applies to building in one's own strength. "When Saul saw any strong man or any valiant man, he took him for himself." Compare this to David's attitude toward God. David allowed the Holy Spirit to send him the future men of valor to the cave of Adullam and thereafter at Ziklag and Hebron. David was content to let the Lord build the house. If our heart is right and God is behind what we are doing, He will send everyone we need to do the work. We don't have to buy people's strength or otherwise strive to attract their ability. God will create the relationships if we are open. Note that many of the mighty men God gave him were not all that attractive at the start (1 Sam 22:2).

If an insecure leader is in the presence of the real anointing or a person with a more agile and understanding mind than his own he will often feel the need to put that person down. Sadly, such a leader cannot bear for someone to surpass him in excellence or achievement (unless he can give the impression that he had something to do with their success). Real fathers, as we have seen, rejoice when their sons surpass them. While we have seen men give lip service to this idea from the pulpit, in action and deed they continue to vie for preeminence, thus quenching the development of those around them.

Ambition imagines vacuums in leadership situations. It mistakes patience and "waiting on the Lord" for a lack of initiative. It is insensitive and will dive right into situations and attempt to fill the imagined vacuum with its own presumptive leadership. It generally sees position as being greater than relationship and will strive for position.

# Ambitious Apostles

In the last thirty years a flurry of apostolic movements have arisen, led by men of God full of fire and zeal. For the most part, these have been spawned by a restoration of the truth of fivefold ministry teams and apostolic-prophetic building teams. This has been a welcome development since the passage in Ephesians 4:11-12 that God gave the ascension ministries for the equipping of the saints is crucial to understanding the church. Unfortunately, while many have been able to clearly articulate the concept, there has been little of the practical working out of the concept in reality. In fact, many who have touted the restoration of the five-fold ministry have often exhibited the most carnal ambition.

In some apostolic networks many young men will follow an ambitious leader because they have nowhere else to go and there is often an exciting and well-articulated vision accompanying the movement. Other young men will follow because of their own ambitious drive. While they may discern the presence of worldly ambition in the leader, they are hoping that by associating with him they will be rewarded for their loyalty and eventually advanced. We have seen men jump on the bandwagon of an apostolic movement in a similar way that people get involved with political movements. As they learn the art of politics they are hoping that their "hour in the sun" will come some day affording them the opportunity to control others. So they vie for the favor of the leader in the hopes of being promoted.

As in political parties, these situations give rise to an inevitable "pecking order" where those who are the most skilled in the art of politics and most willing to perform for the leader are brought into the inner circle. This favoritism breeds discouragement and discontent in the "lower ranks" as certain brethren are overlooked. Those who are not ambitious but rather content to quietly wait upon the Lord are often perceived as being too laid back, passive, or lacking in motivation. Sadly, they are often perceived as lacking in leadership ability and are passed by.

What is the problem in such movements? For one, they thrive on performance much as a secular business does. For another, they often judge men by their charisma and achievement, rather than their character and the fruit of the Spirit. Bible teacher and author DeVern Fromke once said that, "what a man builds with his gift he often destroys with his character." When we are willing to overlook obvious character flaws for the sake of the "work" and the "vision" we are headed for trouble!

## "Bear" Bryant

Several years ago I was at a meeting in Selma, Alabama, at the time when Coach Bryant had just taken over the University of Alabama football program. "Bear" began to tell us what he expected to accomplish and how he would do it. He began to talk about the kind of young men he would recruit. He made a statement I will never forget. He said, "Some of you think that football builds character. Well, I'll tell you right now that I don't plan to waste my time trying to teach character. I want the young men that come into my program to already have good character. I'll teach them how to play football." In the church, we will have compassion on those who have flaws in their character and do all that we can to help them change. We will not reject them from fellowship. But no matter how gifted they are, there is no excuse for overlooking serious character flaws just to get a person's gift involved in the ministry. When it comes to government in the church, it is doubly true.

As the title of this book suggests, the problem is that the church has been lacking in true fathers. Many young men in some of these apostolic networks have been wounded or abandoned by older men who through carelessness or ambition manifested that they were not really fathers. They were tremendously gifted and anointed but did not have the heart and maturity of fathers. The ground is strewn with young men who have been left in the wake of strong men who after using them for their own end, cast them aside.

Gordon Dalbey, in his fantastic book on father/son relationships entitled Father and Son, the Wound, the Healing, the Call to Manhood tells of a joint interview he had with Leonard LeSourd, former editor of Guideposts magazine. LeSourd, a pilot in World War II, had a long and distinguished career as a writer and editor. As Dalbey sat ready for the interview, thoughts came to him which he poignantly expressed in his book:

> "Thus I sat both uncertain and hopeful in the radio studio beside gray-haired Leonard LeSourd. Could I trust this guy? Would he discount me and try to take over? Indeed, would my own longing for a mentor betray me and encourage him to do so?"[1]

I believe this is exactly how many young leaders in the Body of Christ look at older men today. Can older men be trusted not to discount younger men? Will they try to take over? Unfortunately, in many cases, the answer is no to the first question and yes to the second.

## Moving Landmarks

One day while reading in my Bible, Deuteronomy 27:17 jumped off the page:

> "Cursed is the one who moves his neighbor's landmark."

I had preached on the subject of landmarks and had listened to others do so many times. Mostly what I had heard and associated with the idea of landmarks and the warnings in Proverbs about moving them pertained to the necessity of keeping doctrine pure. But this time a new revelation suddenly began to unfold to me.

A landmark in ancient Israel defined one's inheritance. When Jabez asked God to increase his borders or inheritance in 1 Chr. 4:10, the word in Hebrew refers to landmarks, and therefore to his inheritance. He was asking God to increase his inheritance. David said, "the lines have fallen to me in pleasant places" in Ps 16:6, and concludes the verse with a declaration that he indeed had a good inheritance. In stretching the lines to measure an inheritance, they are always stretched from landmark to landmark.

I gave twenty-two years of my life and energy to the building of a church. What was done there, in the Spirit, is part of my inheritance. Please don't misunderstand. I assure you, dear reader, that I understand well that the church belongs to Jesus Christ and not to me. But since it is clear from 2 Cor. 5:10 that "we must all appear before the judgment seat of Christ, that each one may receive what is due to him for the things done while in the body, whether good or bad," then it appears that our inheritance will be good or bad, depending on what we have accomplished for Christ by the Spirit.

Now, just like Jabez (1 Chron. 4:9-10), I have spent my life asking God for a greater spiritual inheritance, and working to gain it. I have tried so far as I know, to work legally.

I was a young lawyer in the rural south in my earlier days. I saw how an unscrupulous lawyer was occasionally able to use cleverness and the ignorance of others to dupe unsuspecting heirs out of their rightful estates. By subterfuge and playing upon ignorance, they were able to move landmarks and gain part of some one else's rightful inheritance. Sometimes this was done using the technicalities of the law. There was one man I observed who did nothing but probate work, looking for opportunities to make dishonest gain in this way.

If you have been in the ministry for very long and have built anything of substance for the Lord, you are aware that there are brethren who will try to move your landmarks and take part of your inheritance if they can. Ambitious men will often try to do this.

When I first had this thought, I fell to my knees and cried out to God. Had I ever moved anyone's landmarks? I want all of the blessing I can get. Like Jabez, I want the hand of God to be with me. When others had tried to move my landmarks and take part of my inheritance, I had gotten angry and incensed. Was I perhaps reaping what I had sowed? God was gracious and pointed out some times when I had been guilty. I was young in the ministry and didn't know what I know now, but nevertheless I was guilty. I repented with all my heart. I told the Lord that if there were any way possible to go back and undo what I had done, I would do it. I meant it! But spilled water cannot be picked up. Like Jabez, I ask God daily to keep me from evil and sinning in this way ever again.

We fathers and those who are called to the apostolic role need to be sowing blessing, not filling the field with curses. Ambition will always cause you to try to move in on another man's inheritance.

## Godly Increase

There are only two legitimate ways to increase your sphere of influence and authority, your inheritance. The first is to do what Jabez did. Ask God to increase your borders. He will gladly do this if your heart motives are right. He will do it by divine encounters, by sending people to you, by giving you revelation, and yes, even by increasing finances. Isaiah 9:7 tells us that there will be no end to the increase of the Lord's government. There is enough authority and territory for everyone that wants it legally. We don't ever have to move anyone else's landmarks. The apostle Paul made it quite clear in Rom 15:20 that he had no desire to build on another man's foundation.

The second way to increase an inheritance legally is by marriage. This speaks of a new relationship where two inheritances are combined, neither party losing anything, but both gaining what the other had. As we relate to each other, the Spirit of God will put some together so that inheritances will be combined. Paul shared in Timothy's inheritance in Christ, and Timothy shared in Paul's.

Wherever and whenever any leader tries to move a landmark in the kingdom of God, I am convinced that a curse will surely come. It can be repented of, but the ripples of mistrust and hurt go out and can not be easily stopped, if at all. We must be terribly careful in these matters of authority, for all authority belongs to Him. Ambition is at the root of all such attempts. Satan tried awfully hard to remove a landmark in the garden. Wrong ambition is devilish indeed.

1. Gordon Dalbey, Father and Son, The Wound, The Healing, The Call to Manhood: Thomas Nelson Publishers, Nashville, TN., 1992, page 174 ff.

# 9

# THE MYSTERY OF LAWLESSNESS

For the mystery of lawlessness is already at work (2 Thess. 2:7)

The Bible reveals that the entire world is surrounded by the mystery of lawlessness. That's because the whole world lies in the power of wickedness (I John 5:19). Unfortunately, the church is not exempt from the influence of wickedness. One expression of lawlessness, anarchy, is very much alive today in the Body of Christ. Since the emergence of the people of God on the earth the mystery of lawlessness has manifested in various forms.

In the book of Judges we see this mystery of lawlessness at work in the hearts of men in the days following the death of Joshua. The writer sums up that period by stating that "every man did what was right in his own eyes" (Judges 17:6). This was certainly a wrong concept, but it was rooted in that mystery of lawlessness which was at work in the earth affecting the people of God.

# Manifestations in the Church

There have been many different manifestations of lawlessness in the Church. One form it has taken in recent decades is in so-called "co-equality" or "co-equal eldership". This is a form of local church leadership in which there is no acknowledged head but a group of "co-equal" elders governing the church. It is interesting to note that after the death of Joshua this is exactly the form of government which led Israel; there was no headship but only elders leading as a group. This was the form of government in place just prior to the total breakdown that led to anarchy at the time of the Judges (Joshua 24). This is far better than anarchy, but when attempted often produces agendas, gridlock, and lack of vision. This is certainly a wrong method and is often spawned by a spirit of lawlessness which rebels against proper authority.

Another expression of lawlessness in the church today is usurpation. This problem was foreseen by the apostle Paul, and he warned the church at Ephesus of its danger (Acts 20:29-30). There have always been men seeking to gain entrance into a church or group of churches with a view to taking over leadership or cutting away individuals from ordained authority. It is usually the ambitious who succumb to these men and follow them. Perhaps the Lord uses these men to weed out of the church those whose hearts easily go astray. Nevertheless, the resulting trauma caused by these men is painful and often cripples the work of God. The divisions which these men cause can impede for years the faith of those who are weak or who are babes in Christ.

## A Story of Usurpation

There was a dear apostolic man in a foreign land. After twenty years of faithful work, the Lord had put together several wonderful churches and the anointing and blessing were rising steadily. As is so often the case, the evidences of successful ministry began to attract those who wanted to partake of the fruit. Many came in integrity because they saw the apostolic anointing on the brother. Others came only because they saw ministry opportunities and because of a desire to eat from the tree. Like David in 1 Chr. 12: 17, my friend welcomed them all . He was a careful but accepting man, willing to let the Holy Spirit do the sorting.

One of the new men that came into the group had a big church and a very charismatic presence. It was clear from the beginning that he came with ideas of leadership that didn't always include the faithful apostolic brother. At about this time a large and expanding apostolic network also moved in, attracted by the work that had been done and desiring that the faithful apostolic man would join with them along with the several churches that he had pioneered and attracted. He understood after a few months that a pyramidal organization was being built rather than solid relationships. When he resisted the efforts to make him a part of the large organization, they went elsewhere, but took with them both the charismatic leader with the large church and one other church. Both of these churches were among the wealthiest and most promising in terms of numbers and income, but not necessarily the most promising in the Spirit.

Upon being confronted about going in and dividing the little apostolic network that was developing so nicely, the answer was given that 'they didn't divide the work but the ambition of the charismatic leader who followed them away divided the work." Now this was actually a true analysis of what happened. But lawlessness and ambition in the heart of one man will call unto lawlessness and ambition in the heart of another man, just as "deep calls unto deep." The damage was done. Relationships were strained. The work was temporarily weakened. Also it should be noted here that the larger group which enticed the two churches to follow them had the seeds of destruction within and eventually had their own problems.

Many pastors will accept disgruntled members from other churches from the same town or neighborhood without question. This is tantamount to encouraging lawlessness. Often it transfers sin and lawlessness from one group or church to another. May the Lord give us faithful people and fellow workers who will not succumb to the spirit of lawlessness.

## God's Gift of Leaders

It is clear that one of the reasons God gives leaders is to safeguard the church from the spirit of lawlessness. That's because true leaders will keep the saints properly directed to the true Shepherd rather than to themselves. This is exactly what the apostle Paul said about those who try to usurp authority in the Body of Christ "in order to draw away disciples after them" (Acts 20:27).

Just as the Father gave the Son (John 3:16), the Son in turn gave to the Church certain gifts, the so-called "five-fold ministry" (Ephesians 4:11). Its purpose is to form, equip and guide the church, to serve the church, and to bring it to maturity so it can fulfill its God-given destiny and purpose. These gifted men are anointed for that purpose and have true authority from heaven. It stands to reason, therefore, that one of the results of their ministry is to cause the hearts of men to be tested as does all authority which comes down from above. For example, true apostolic authority will often bring out rebellion in hearts; not solely for the purpose of exposing it but that in exposing it it might be put away. When the authority of God is exercised properly by apostles it should have the effect of destroying all rebellion against the King that exists in the Body of Christ. I say this because Ephesians 4 is partly lifted from Ps 68:18 which says that:

"Thou hast ascended on high, thou hast led captivity captive, thou hast received gifts for men, yea, for the rebellious also, that the Lord might dwell among them." (KJV)

It is vital to see the importance of apostles in this regard. The Holy Spirit raises up elders and other ministries in the Church (Acts 20:28), but Christ Himself personally calls apostles (and the other five-fold ministry gifts). Several passages make it clear that the apostle is called directly by Christ (Romans 1:1, I Cor. 1:1, II Timothy 1:11). It also seems to indicate that there is a witness among the people (or at least should be) when they are taught to recognize a true apostle.

According to the apostle Paul, the very foundation of the church  is placed by the apostolic-prophetic team (Ephesians. 2:20; 3:5). With the office comes the anointing to function in that particular sphere which is given by Christ. Yet it cannot be acquired by study or obtaining degrees or even by prayer. It is supernatural, not natural. It may be accompanied with administrative or executive ability, but often is not. Worldly ability has no bearing on the anointing, but may enhance and adorn it if ability is present and subservient to the anointing. It comes from Jesus Christ and is part of the overall anointing which flows from Him. The early church was built upon apostolic doctrine and anointing, and New Testament churches must continue to be built on that doctrine and anointing today. For Christ is the same yesterday, today and forever.

That is not to say that any new apostolic doctrine is being formed today, for it is not. At the close of the book of Revelation the apostle John warns that no one should add or subtract from the words of the book (Rev. 22:18-19). There is no doubt that the

Holy Spirit is referring to the Word of God, canonized much later but known to Him even then. What is written in Scripture is all that there is to be written and no apostle was to come along to add or take away anything from the written revelation.

While honest men have struggled for almost two thousand years over certain interpretations of that Word, it doesn't change the nature of that Word. There is room for honest differences between those of good heart. What we can be assured of is that the Holy Spirit will lead us into all truth before it is all over if we remain honest, teachable, and humble.

God demands that apostles, above all other ministries, exhibit a lack of guile as a necessary ingredient of their ministry. Among the many aspects of our ministry which Paul so beautifully outlines he lists as number one:

> "But we have renounced the hidden things of shame, not walking in craftiness nor handling the word of God deceitfully, but by manifestation of the truth commending ourselves to every man's conscience in the sight of God."
> 2 Cor. 4:2

## The Problem of False Apostles

Last but not least of the problems in the modern church associated with lawlessness is that of false apostles. According to the apostle Paul in II Cor.. 11:13-15, false apostles are not only deceitful workers, but agents of Satan himself (even though perhaps unwittingly). These men sought glory, money, and authority for themselves as well as preached false doctrine not in keeping with the sound doctrine upon which the church is built.

It is no wonder that in commending the church at Ephesus, the risen Christ pointed out the fact that they "cannot bear those who are evil. And you have tested those who say they are apostles and are not, and have found them liars" (Revelation 2:2).

Only true apostles can lay out, plant, and maintain true church foundations. If the foundation is not true the building will be skewed.

I am blessed with two sons who are building contractors. A few years ago one of them was hired by a desperate contractor who had just fired his framing subcontractor. The building frame was up and the roof was on when it was discovered that the whole building was badly out of plumb. My son was hired to see if he could possibly fix it. It was comical, heroic and sad, all at the same time, to see them pulling and tugging on the walls of that building. They loosened certain parts of the wall. They had two heavy pick up trucks chained to sections of the wall pulling to move the walls but not break them. After a full day's work, they had it almost plumb, enough to pass inspection. Had the foundation been off, it would have been impossible to correct the problem.

As any contractor will tell you, it is difficult, if not impossible, to correct a building already constructed upon a skewed foundation. But let us not despair! All is not lost. The Holy Spirit is a Contractor who can shore up a foundation, even after construction of the building has begun. Yet He uses true apostles and true prophets to do the job.

# 10

# THE NEED FOR HELP

A story told by an old man years ago down in Eastern North Carolina illustrates the mentality of some brethren. He told of a farmer who lived on an island in the Roanoke River. This old farmer was very proud of his island for it had excellent land for growing crops. He lived there alone with his chickens, cows and dogs on a beautiful farm.

One day a group from up the river came to see him to warn him of an impending flood. "There has been torrential rains up in the hills and the flood is coming this way. Get off the island while you still can!" The old man refused to budge, saying he would stick it out on his island. He had been there all of his life and had survived floods before. Besides, he knew the Lord wouldn't let him down.

The Lord would protect him.

The river rose steadily until the old man had to get on his roof. A neighbor came by in a rowboat and offered to take him off the island, which was by now under water. The old man refused saying , "The Lord will not let me down, He will save me! Praise the Lord."

An hour or so later another neighbor came by in a power boat and the same scenario developed. Again the old man insisted the Lord would save him. Finally a national guard helicopter arrived and offered to swing him from the roof which was now within an inch or two of being totally submerged. Again the answer was the same, "The Lord will save me."

Several minutes later the old man was swept to his death by drowning. Upon reaching heaven, he reproached the Lord. "I put all my faith in you and you didn't save me" was his embittered accusation. With wonderful patience the Lord looked him right in the eye and said, "I heard you, and I sent three people to save you, but you refused."

We have to want help and be humble enough to foster the relationships that will provide covering and help in the time of need. Fortunately, there are many lone pastors and independent brethren in the Kingdom today who are sincerely looking for fellowship and identity. This is undoubtedly a result of the moving of the Spirit of God. Many have come to understand their vulnerability in standing alone and that real effectiveness is the result of being part of a larger group. Thus, the Spirit of God is creating a great yearning for unity and this is certainly a good thing.

Scripture gives many examples of the importance of working with others as well as the dangers inherent in remaining alone. Perhaps the most poignant example though is found in the book of Judges and the story of the people of Laish:

"So they...went to Laish, to a people quiet and secure; and they struck them with the edge of the sword and burned the city with fire. There was no deliverer, because it was far from Sidon, and they had no ties with anyone" (Judges 18:27-28). Emphasis mine

The people of Laish were peaceful, minding their own business and by all accounts were independent and happy. Undoubtedly, they never considered that a day would come when they would need help from outside. Yet that day did dawn and there was no deliverance, because they were far from help (Sidon) and they had no ties with anyone.

Scripture is clear that the more dedicated a man is and the more aligned with God's purposes the more the enemy will target him. This is especially true for leaders and their churches. He will attack wherever he finds a weak point, unhealed wound or unconfessed sin. Satan and his demonic forces hate the Church and every believer in it.

One of the ways God has ordered for our protection from the enemy is to receive help from the brethren. The Body of Christ is made up of many parts, gifts, and levels of understanding. The members of the Body need each other (see I Corinthians 12:14-26 and Ephesians 4:7-16). These Scriptures are to be fulfilled in each local church as the members function together and through local five-fold ministry relationships.

Yet even though we are technically members of the Body, we can be alone in the battle. When David sought Uriah's death he devised a plan whereby he would die in battle by the hand of the enemy (II Samuel 11:14-15). David knew he could achieve Uriah's death by ordering him into the gate where the battle was fiercest and simultaneously ordering Joab to withdraw support from around him. Like a lamb cut off from the flock, Uriah's fate was sealed. Chances are slim for our survival if we are alone in the midst of the battle. Yet that is exactly the situation that many leaders find themselves in today—alone in the midst of the battle.

As a positive example, Saul's first act as king of Israel was to rally all Israel to save the men of Jabesh-Gilead (I Samuel 11). These men, surrounded by the enemy, in desperation sent messages to their brethren to come and help them. They knew they were part of Israel and that if they asked their brethren would come to help them. What an example of the Body of Christ in action! A great deliverance was wrought as the men of Jabesh-Gilead recognized their limitation and called upon their brethren to help.

Another good example can be seen in the life of David. During his lifetime, David faced many power struggles as well as betrayal by those closest to him; his son Absalom, his son Adonijah, and his cousin, Joab. Yet because he had established a strong father-son relationship with his mighty men they faithfully served him in his time of need. At one point they even rescued him from the giants who would certainly have killed him (II Sam. 15:21). David's relationships with his mighty men are not only a key lesson on the value of being a good leader, but of the need to be rightly related to others in order to take and maintain a kingdom.

Perhaps the writer of Ecclesiastes summed it up best:

> "Two are better than one, because they have a good reward for their labor. For if they fall, one will lift up his companion. But woe to him who is alone when he falls, for he has no one to help him up. Again, if two lie down together, they will keep warm; but how can one be warm alone? Though one may be overpowered by another, two can withstand him. And a threefold cord is not quickly broken" (Ecc, 4: 9-12)

In recent years, we have all bemoaned the poor witness of the nationally known ministers who have become public spectacles. As a result, many pastors have said, "If only he had had a relationship with someone who could speak into his life." Yet very often the fallen brother was proud, independent or cynical and even in crisis and could not see the value of counsel and real cover. If he had, he might have avoided falling so hard.

## The Danger of Independence

There are many pastors and leaders today who, while recognizing their need for fellowship, don't really want any close relationships that might involve commitment on any level. Some of them have had horrible experiences in the past relating to legal or ambitious men who used them or their churches for their own self-aggrandizement. Many just don't see any need for help or are too proud to admit they don't know everything. Or they might just have that good old American spirit so aptly exemplified by Frank Sinatra's classic theme song, My Way.

But, let us return to Laish. When those who came to Laish to conquer it arrived, this is how they saw the inhabitants of the district:

> "So the five men departed and went to Laish. They saw the people who were there, how they dwelt safely, in the manner of the Sidonians, quiet and secure. There were no rulers in the land who might put them to shame for anything. They were far from the Sidonians, and they had no ties with anyone" (Judg. 18:7)

What a picture of a confident people feeling safe and secure with no need for anyone else. There were no rulers (magistrates) in the land to which they were accountable. They had no outside relationships. They lived "like" the Sidonians, but they were far away and had no relationship or accountability to them or anyone. And the truth is, no one else had a relationship or was accountable to them either! No wonder they were such an easy prey.

The fact that the people of Laish dwelt alone and therefore perished is not meant to suggest that outside help will always save the day. Yet it is God's best that we receive help from one another since none of us have all the insights necessary to solve every problem. Nor do we have the ability to perform every task. Solomon said: "Where no counsel is, the people fall; but in the multitude of counselors there is safety." (Proverbs 11:14) There are special people that God puts into our lives to help us develop in the natural; parents, teachers, coaches, Marine Corp drill instructors, mentors in business and the like (the two men in the boats and the national guard helicopter.) Our progress nearly always depends on our ability to receive, assimilate and put into practice what they can teach us. In the same way, God gives us others to help us develop spiritually as well. Just as natural development depends on the assistance of others, so life in God requires those special relationships to guide us in the way. Why would God want us to be independent in our spiritual development? We need to earnestly seek and be open to those special relationships that God provides so that we can receive the maximum benefit in our spiritual journey.

## Thwarting What God is Doing

Today one of God's provisions to enable churches to avoid being like the men of Laish is the emergence of apostolic networks: groupings of churches working together under apostolic leadership and direction. All across the earth these networks have sprung up promising to provide local churches with spiritual covering and protection.

From time to time, we have received invitations from various groups to join and become part of them. Usually, the invitation will come from the key man around which this particular group is forming. While many of these networks are legitimate, often they are raw attempts to take advantage of the vulnerability of lonely men and gain their money and allegiance.

Often, men will thwart what God is attempting to do by taking God's idea and running with it in the flesh. In my own day there have been several legitimate moves of the Holy Spirit which have been thwarted or soiled by overly zealous and ambitious men.

For instance, God really wants discipleship and genuine authority established among his people today. Yet many are wary of pastoral and apostolic oversight because of excesses they experienced in previous movements in earlier decades. The same is true of prosperity and faith. There is no doubt that God intends to bless His people. But because of the excesses of a few men and women who lacked understanding and proper balance in the Word of God, the Church is leery of the prosperity and word-faith movements and will not even examine the merit in what these brethren have to offer. This is unfortunate since many of the brethren from that camp know how to access the Spirit of God by faith much better than some of us who have resisted their teachings.

The same is true of prophets. God certainly wants to restore real prophets in the church today. However so much presumption and weirdness has attended the restoration of the prophetic that many reject it. Some even fear it. Many prophets seem to be unaccountable to anyone on earth for their excesses.

In our day, God desires to restore true apostolic ministry and father-son relationship. But once again, men are taking the ball and running with it in a carnal way! In the next part of this book we will go to the Scriptures to look in a very positive way at the heart of the apostle. Suffice it to say for now that it is extremely urgent that we who are in leadership do not let this golden opportunity to respond to the Holy Spirit drown in the cesspools of ambition, opportunity, or greed.

# 11

# VERTICAL VERSUS HORIZONTAL RELATIONSHIPS

Throughout the world today, there is a great emphasis on promulgating unity among pastors and churches in a given locality. This movement is undoubtedly a work of the Holy Spirit and has produced much fruit in many places. Local pastors in a great number of cities meet regularly for worship and prayer, and are organizing joint worship, evangelistic and youth ventures. Many are overcoming historical denominational barriers, as well as cultural and racial barriers, in order to present a unified face to the principalities, powers, and the unsaved.

These pastor to pastor and church to church relationships in cities and localities may be best described as horizontal relationships. They are occurring despite differences of background, origin, vision and doctrine. They are beneficial in many ways, but especially in the fact that they tend to pool the strengths and gifts of the local churches with the result that much more is accomplished in the Kingdom locally than before.

The church in the New Testament was almost always addressed by the apostles in geographic terms. Regional groupings of churches can develop young leaders and launch them into national and international ministries through their various vertical connections (which we will discuss in a moment). When trouble occurs, these churches are in a better position to help each other quickly. A lot of good work in and for the Kingdom of God is accomplished through these horizontal relationships.

## Vertical Relationships

On the other hand, the New Testament reveals that there are vertical relationships as well as horizontal. These involve authority, oversight, protection, identity and those distinctions which make us different from each other. They include varying kinds of vision, cultural backgrounds, denominational origins, and the like. They also include father-son relationships. Perhaps one simple way of viewing this is that horizontal relationships are regional, neighbor-to-neighbor relationships while vertical are essentially "family." Churches and leaders have always had a tendency to organize vertically because of background, history, doctrine, relationships and vision.

Unfortunately, because of lack of true fathers and the resulting "plastic" vertical relationships, in many situations the ministry and quasi-covering that takes place in the horizontal relationships are far more meaningful to some struggling young leaders than those encountered in the vertical.

It is quite obvious that both types of relationships are good and are in the plan of God. Paul's relationships to Timothy, to Titus, to many others, and to the churches he planted and nurtured were essentially vertical in nature. The trip to Jerusalem in Acts 15 to settle the legalism question worked through vertical relationships. Paul's and Barnabas' relationship to the church at Antioch was vertical. The relationship of the men of Jabesh-Gilead to Saul was vertical (I Samuel 11:1-11), and this is indeed what saved them from their enemies when the crisis came.

In the Corinthian letter, the apostle Paul gives instructions regarding "when the whole church comes together in one place" (I Corinthians 14:23). We know that the early church consisted of many house churches and Paul's instructions undoubtedly applied to those times when all of those house churches would come together. The early church is most often addressed geographically; i.e.. the church at Laodicea, the church at Colossae, the church at Cenchrea, the church at Rome, etc. This implies horizontal relationships.

## Holding Both in Balance

The will of God is that we hold both types of relationships in balance. We must receive what is passed down through the apostolic fathers and teams through vertical relationships.

"And the things that you have heard from me among many witnesses, commit these to faithful men who will be able to teach others also"
(II Timothy 2:2)

In this vertical relationship, Timothy was to take what he received from the apostle Paul and pass it on to others. This is clearly a vertical relationship. Paul also told Timothy to "stir up the gift of God which is in you through the laying on of my hands", another clear reference to the vertical kind of relationship. It is clear that vertical relationships were vital in the ministry of the apostle Paul.

The danger always lies in sacrificing one set of relationships for the other. To exalt or over emphasize any of God's truths or ministry or callings or gifts is to be out of balance, and will always have to be dealt with by Him. In the father-son relationship there is a blessing that involves strengthening, covering, identity, and protection which cannot be substituted by horizontal relationships. It is a spiritual matter, not an intellectual one. It is a question of what God will do through the relationship, not what man will do.

Do you see why it is so important that there be real fathers and real apostles in the Body of Christ? If there are not, then a unique and certain channel of blessing, unity and strength is missing. A true apostle will encourage his sons to form greater and greater horizontal relationships while doing everything possible to strengthen vertical relationships at the same time.

It is time to draw the horizontal circle bigger, not smaller. I have never forgotten a poem my wife introduced to me some fifty years ago that neatly expresses what our attitude should be:

"He drew a circle that shut me out…
Heretic, rebel, a thing to flout…
But love and I had the wit to win…
We drew a circle that took him in!"

Anonymous

# Part 4

•

# THE HEART OF AN APOSTLE

# 12

# THE ACTIVE MARKS
# OF AN APOSTLE

*"I know your works , your labor, your patience, and
that you cannot bear those who are evil. And you
have tested those who say they are apostles and
are not, and have found them liars."*

*Rev. 2:2*

In the book of Revelation, the Lord commended the Church of
Ephesus for their discernment of true and false apostles. If we are
to follow the Lord in this and receive his commendation, we also
must be able to recognize and test true and false apostles. When
we come to Scripture there are many evidences given of what true
apostles are like and how they should behave. In this part of the
book we will examine carefully the marks of a true apostle extract-
ing from Scripture a biblical portrait of this all-important ministry.

Much has been written recently about the functioning of an
apostle, thereby defining the apostle by his function. Much has
been written defining the office by looking at historical models and
shadows in the Old Testament. I do not want to approach this sub-

ject from those well worn angles. There are plenty of good books already written in that vein. Rather, I would like to discern what characterizes an apostle from the inside out. What should be his recognizable heart motivation. God, after all, is more concerned with the heart than with the outward appearance. What should an apostle look like in the light of what we have said so far about fathers. There is no question that Paul equates being an apostle with being a father when we coordinate the verses in 1 Cor. 4:9 and 15 with those in between:

> For I think that God has displayed us, the apostles, last, as men con-
> demned to death; for we have been made a spectacle to the world, both
> to angels and to men. We are fools for Christ's sake, but you are wise
> in Christ! We are weak, but you are strong! You are distinguished, but
> we are dishonored! To the present hour we both hunger and thirst, and
> we are poorly clothed, and beaten, and homeless. And we labor, work-
> ing with our own hands. Being reviled, we bless; being persecuted, we
> endure; being defamed, we entreat. We have been made as the filth
> of the world, the offscouring of all things until now. I do not write
> these things to shame you, but as my beloved children I warn you. For
> though you might have ten thousand instructors in Christ, yet you do
> not have many fathers; for in Christ Jesus I have begotten you through
> the gospel." Emphasis mine.

Before I proceed any further, I feel I should make the following distinction. I maintain that an apostle should certainly be a father. That is a major thrust of this book. However, lest there should be a question in some minds, I state here that there are without question some fathers who are called to be pastors, as well as other five fold ministries. Are all fathers apostles? No, there are father-pastors shepherding churches. There are father-apostles exercising author-ity over pastors and churches. Not all ministers are fathers, but all apostles should be fathers.

Some of the traits of true apostles I have characterized as external and overt. These I have referred to as the "active" marks of the apostle. Others might be classified as "inward" or internal; that is, they lie within the heart. Yet while they lie within they do produce an outward witness. Therefore, I refer to them as the apostle's "witness" and have devoted the entirety of the next chapter to describing them.

Anyone calling himself an apostle (or called that by others) should have some measure of these qualities evident in his life and ministry. That is not to say that everyone who has the apostolic mantle will necessarily embody all of these to the greatest degree. However there must be some modicum of evidence in his life of these qualities if he is to be substantiated as a true apostle. That is not to say that we will all agree upon who is and who isn't an apostle. Even the apostle Paul was not considered an apostle by some (I Corinthians 9:1-2). This was undoubtedly due in part to the fact that he did not have a relationship with them, so that they were unable to see and receive his apostolic character, gift and heart. In any case, we must be able to discern, like the Ephesian church, those who are true apostles in our midst.

## Marks of an Apostle: In the Word

A true apostle should have the ability to teach, impart, and set a good doctrinal foundation into a church (Acts 2:42; I Cor. 3:9-10, Ephesians 2:20). This should not be confused with preaching ability. Preaching is a glorious gift and greatly to be desired, but we are talking about more than just stirring emotions and building up souls. Yet neither should we confuse it with the recitation of cold, sterile doctrine fit only for the intellect. Intellect speaks to intellect as deep calls unto deep. The foundation truth of God must be set in place by the power of the Spirit, not the power of the intellect.

That is not ever to say that good doctrine is to be ignored. But the Spirit and the Word must be combined so that the Spirit is somehow in the Word. In this way, the foundation is laid by the Spirit as He uses the apostle.

This ability combines the Gospel (I Corinthians 9:16-17) and all its elements with other foundational teaching. This would include repentance from dead works, faith toward God, the doctrine of baptisms, the laying on of hands, the resurrection of the dead and eternal judgment (Heb. 6:1-2). It also involves the revelation of the King and His kingdom. This is essentially what comprised the 'apostle's doctrine' referred to in Acts 2:42. Within these subjects a whole range of other topics are certainly available to be covered. Yet these must always be taught within the physical and spiritual parameters of Scripture. When these parameters are widened, narrowed or in any way not strictly observed, so that something is either added or taken away from Scripture, it will inevitably endanger the faith of the believers, as well as the foundation of he church. The foundation will be skewed and God's blessing will never rest on it fully.

One might ask at this point, "What is the difference between the apostle and the teacher in these particular endeavors?" The answer is that there is little difference in quality or quantity. The teacher's gift enables him or her to bring clarity to Scripture in such a way that people gain understanding and receive revelation. In doing so he adds to and strengthens the foundation. The difference between the apostle and the teacher is in the supernatural, governmental anointing of the apostle to set the foundation in place. The teacher does not have an overlying grace to place things in position with relevance to other things. Often he does not see the joining of prophetic input to the teaching input or the evangelistic input, or the pastoral input.

In many ways, the man called to be a pastor is similar to the apostle. He is anointed to see things fit together in application to the welfare of the local church since he is gifted to see its effect in the church. I have often thought that the pastoral gift is simply local, whereas the apostolic is both local and trans-local. The pastor is primarily locally oriented, whereas the apostle is primarily Kingdom and world oriented. In my travels, I have met many local pastors who are apostles in the making. In His time, God will spread their tents so that their influence will reach far beyond their own local sphere.

There is another thing that must be understood pertaining to the measure which God gives to each man. In Deuteronomy the Lord tells us that there are "captains of ten, fifties, hundreds and thousands" (Deut. 1:15). Some men are only captains of tens. They make wonderful home group leaders. Others are captains of fifties and hundreds and can handle the situations and duties that occur in smaller groups and smaller churches. They are not to be lightly esteemed, for they are just as important to the kingdom of God as the grandest pastor of the largest church in Paris, London or Los Angeles. Others are captains of thousands. The Lord Himself knows our abilities. He will not allow a captain of thousands to be wasted unless there is some personal lack of cooperation with the Holy Spirit that limits God's willingness to use him. To put a captain of tens or hundreds over thousands would be cruel indeed. It is a good thing to realistically  assess one's limitations.

The five-fold gifts are important and greatly complement each other. Yet the apostle's vision is broader than the others. It includes an anointing to bring things together. It also entails an anointing, not only to place the foundation, but also to see that others are doing it properly. When allowed by local authority, he has an ability to make corrections in a faulty foundation and should be able to do so with a minimum amount of destruction and trauma to the church.

# Marks of an Apostle: The Acts

Is it fair today to expect that apostles perform signs and wonders as they did in the early church? We won't say very much about this as it really falls in the realm of function. However, a few thoughts are in order here.

> "And through the hands of the apostles many sings and wonders were done among the people. And they were all with one accord in Solomon's Porch" (Acts 5:12).

and,

> "Then fear came upon every soul, and many wonders and signs were done through the apostles" (Acts 2:43)

Perhaps it will be helpful to first define what signs and wonders are. According to Thayer's Definitions of Strong's Concordance, a sign is as follows:

> "a sign, a mark, a token; a) that by which a person or a thing is distinguished from others and is known; b) a sign, a prodigy, a portent, that is, an unusual occurrence, transcending the common course of nature: 1) used of signs portending remarkable events soon to happen; 2) used of miracles and wonders by which God authenticates the men sent by him, or by which men prove that the cause they are pleading is God's cause.."

A wonder, according to the same source is "1) a prodigy, a portent; 2) a miracle; performed by anyone."

It is clear from the record in Acts that healing, deliverance, salvation, and outpourings of the Holy Spirit followed the apostles wherever they went. And it is not a stretch to say that such signs should be occurring regularly to authenticate true apostles today. I say regularly for the following reason. While we can read the Book of Acts in approximately two or three hours it covers about twenty-five or thirty years of activity. The miracles we see in Acts were not necessarily occurring daily. Since the presence of the Lord was so abundant in the early church, there is no doubt that a sign like the deaths of Ananias and Saphira were very spectacular, but not necessarily a daily or even a yearly occurrence. As far as we know this particular sign only occurred once.

We do see many great miracles and signs occurring in the world today. If all these were compressed into twenty-eight chapters of a book we might get the impression that there is one occurring every second. However, this would not necessarily be the case. Though many signs and wonders do accompany modern apostles they are not all super-spectacular in nature, nor need they be to confirm the office. Yet that being said, there should be something supernatural and wonderful at times attending apostolic ministry. If there is nothing at all, we should stand back and wonder if there is indeed an apostle at work!

## Marks of an Apostle: Impartation of Gifts

"And when Simon saw that through the laying of on the apostles' hands the Holy Spirit was given, he offered them money." Acts 8:18

In this passage in the book of Acts the apostles were sent to Samaria by the brethren at Jerusalem to supplement the work of the evangelist Philip. While Philip's powerful evangelistic ministry had brought them to Christ, the Holy Spirit had not yet fallen on the new believers there. When the apostles arrived they began laying hands on the believers who then received the baptism in the Holy Spirit. A similar occurrence is recorded in Acts 19:1-6 when Paul met the twelve men near Ephesus who were believers. After laying hands on them they also received the Holy Spirit and spoke with tongues and prophesied.

From the record in Acts it appears that people received the baptism in the Holy Spirit either directly from Christ (as at Pentecost) or at the hands of the apostles. This is by all means a special sign that should be a part of the apostolic equipment. Many should receive the Baptism in the Holy Spirit at the hands of true apostles.

Paul refers to a gift imparted to his young son Timothy when he had laid his hands on him:

> "Therefore, I remind you to stir up the gift of God which is in you through the laying on of my hands." II Timothy 1:6

Most likely he was referring to the same time that the presbyters (elders) had laid hands on Timothy, since Paul mentions it he was present (I Timothy 4:14). The implication is that something special happened when Paul laid his hands on Timothy. Without belaboring the point, it is obvious that something real is imparted when an apostle lays his hand, by the Spirit, on a young leader. Whatever Timothy received he was called to stir it up especially in times of necessity.

## Marks of an Apostle: Authority

All authority is from God (Romans 13:1). Without question the Bible teaches that the only rightful power within creation is ultimately that of the Creator. All authority on earth is delegated from above and man is accountable for its use, whether he believes it or not.

Apostolic authority is delegated authority and it is delegated for the purpose of building the church:

> "For even if I should boast somewhat more about our authority, which the Lord gave us for edification and not for your destruction."
>
> II
> Cor. 10:8

Apostolic authority is delegated from above and should be used only for building up and not tearing down. To flow properly it must be funneled through solid relationships. Otherwise it always results in legalism. It does not flow well without the relationship. Paul said,

> "Am I not an apostle? Am I not free? Have I not seen Jesus Christ our Lord? Are you not my work in the Lord? If I am not an apostle to others, yet doubtless I am to you. For you are the seal of my apostleship in the Lord." (1 Cor. 9:1-2)

I think we all recognize the existence of apostolic oversight and authority. But we can see that it exists in some cases and not in others (vs. 2). The exercise of authority is based on involvement and serving, not on position. There is "governmental apostleship" based on such relationship and involvement which has to be recognized and agreed to by the saints being governed. The apostle is not responsible to make authority work, but the saints are! Since true submission to authority can only come from the heart, a solid relationship of trust, worthiness and friendship has to be in place. There is also an "ministerial apostleship" which does not have to involve any oversight whatsoever. Recognizing someone as having the gift of an apostle does not necessarily confer authority over lives and situations.

# Alexander

Plutarch tells a story about Alexander the Great. Alexander lived from 356 to 323 B.C.. He is recognized as one of the greatest leaders of all time. He conquered and exercised tremendous authority over most of the known world before he died at the age of 33. This story is retold by Bill Bennett₁ and illustrates how authority is fulfilled and flows in service and relationship rather than position.

> "Alexander the Great was leading his army homeward after his great victory against Porus in India. The country through which they now marched was bare and desert and his army suffered dreadfully from heat, hunger, and, most of all, thirst. The soldiers' lips cracked and their throats burned from want of water, and many were ready to lie down and give up.
>
> About noon one day the army met a party of Greek travelers. They were on mules and carried with them vessels filled with water. One of them, seeing the king almost choking from thirst, filled a helmet and offered it to him.
>
> Alexander took it in his hands, then looked around at the faces of his suffering soldiers, who craved refreshment just as much as he did.
>
> "Take it away," he said, "for if I drink alone the rest will be out of heart, and you have not enough for all."
>
> So he handed the water back without touching a drop of it. And the soldiers, cheering their king, leaped to their feet, and demanded to be led forward."

Even though the apostle must sometimes "root out and pull down" as well as bring correction, the motive behind godly authority is always to encourage and build up the church and its people.

If correction is not followed up by encouragement and rebuilding, it is doubtful that authority was properly exercised.

Authority is also limited. Paul says as much in 2 Cor. 10:13-15:

> "We, however, will not boast beyond measure, but within the limits of the sphere which God appointed us—a sphere which especially includes you. For we are not overextending ourselves (as though our authority did not extend to you), for it was to you that we came with the gospel of Christ"

Notice Paul mentions not boasting "beyond measure, but within the limits of the sphere" God had appointed him. To go beyond the measure of one's authority is to be ambitious for self. It is always demonic in nature and produces a negative reaction in the body of Christ. Paul ends chapter ten of First Corinthians with the admonition, "But he who glories, let him glory in the Lord, For not he who commends himself is approved, but whom the Lord commends (2 Cor.. 10:17-18). Seeking authority beyond one's measure (or what the Lord has clearly given) is always an attempt at self-glorification.[2] It is the basis of false apostleship about which we are warned in Revelation 2:2.2 Self-promotion is clearly Satanic in principle and lies at the heart of his own attempt at self-exaltation above the throne of God.

It goes without saying that to boast beyond one's measure is also evidence of the flesh. Contrast that with Paul's own testimony regarding the manner in which he walked while among the Corinthians:

> "For our boasting is this: the testimony of our conscience that we conducted ourselves in the world in simplicity and godly sincerity, not with fleshly wisdom but by the grace of God, and more abundantly toward you. For we are not writing any other things to you than what you read

or understand. Now I trust you will understand, even to the end."

(2 Cor.. 1:12-13)

What a difference between the way the apostle carried himself while with them and those super-apostles who had seduced them by their own boasting and self-aggrandizement! Simplicity and godly sincerity demanded that the apostle walk humbly, not boasting in himself and his own achievements in contrast to those false apostles whose authority was based in their own fleshly claims.

This heart attitude included the refusal on Paul's part to attempt to control others or interfere with their faith:

> "Not that we would have dominion over your faith, but are fellow workers for your joy: for by faith you stand"(2 Cor.. 1:24).

Paul understood that every individual in the Body of Christ must walk by his or her own faith, for this is the only way to Christian maturity and to pleasing God. According to Paul, this is the role of the apostle (and for the rest of the five-fold ministry): that through them the church might be brought to maturity so that it pleases God in every way (Eph. 4:13-15). To exercise dominion over anyone's faith is to hold them back from maturing in the same way that a parent who keeps a child from stumbling and falling down hinders that child from learning to walk.

In the passage quoted above, Paul makes it clear that the goal of ministry is to be fellow-workers promoting the saint's joy, while refusing to take dominion over their faith. While he deals strongly with the Corinthian's problems in no uncertain terms, even exercising authority to turn a sinful man over to Satan, he does not take dominion over their faith. His way is to send them word, hoping that upon hearing they will be obedient (2 Cor. 2:9). Now this was certainly a risky affair. What if the church had not responded?

The fact is they did respond. The foundation that the apostle had laid was good. He could trust that the Holy Spirit would witness to his words and work in the hearts of the people and their leaders. A great deal more about this will be said in Chapter 13 under the heading of "Confidence in Christ."

Too many times I have seen apostolic fathers rush in at the first sign of major trouble, take the authority out of the hands of the local leadership and attempt to control the outcome. This may seem like the safest way to protect apostolic reputation, but it is certainly not the Pauline way. It also is not the way of insuring that the saints achieve maturity.

Years ago, during a severe governmental crisis in a wonderful church where I was asked to help out, I was receiving phone calls almost daily from brethren who had an interest in the outcome. Some of these calls were rather intimidating in nature and insisted that I "do something." One call came in late one night from a prophetic brother who had quite a bit of clout in the Christian world as well as in our situation. He told me that "everything was falling apart, that if I didn't do something he was going to step in, find someone with some authority, and get something done, and that if it all fell apart, that I was going to get the blame." I told him as calmly as I could that it was apparent from his own statement that he recognized his own lack of authority, and that it would probably be better if he stayed out of the whole situation. I already knew of a solution working in the wings and within a few days the Lord supplied the answer to the problem and everyone saw the Lord's hand at work rather than mine. When the answer became obvious I then had to take some action to put it into effect, but nevertheless it was clearly the Lord's answer. To this day the people in that church have confidence in me because of the outcome in that situation. The people are always strengthened when they see the Lord work. They are also more willing in the long run to follow leaders who demonstrate that they can hear the Lord and are willing to let Him work.

When men rush in to take over churches with deep problems, changing pastors and elders abruptly and arbitrarily, they damage people's faith as well as relationships. There are many churches no longer in existence because of this kind of brash action on the part of apostles. This is due in part to the fact that some apostolic men are so afraid of failure and the possible damage to their own reputations that they move too quickly to abort churches. They will only give their real time and efforts to successful churches so as to avoid any risk of failure. Only God has the right to put a church to death since only He can bring it to birth. In the case where a church is sick or in danger, the father apostle's job is to hold its hand; not to pull the life support plug himself. Obviously there may come a time to walk away, but Christ will make it abundantly clear when that time has arrived. There should never be any guessing.

I have seen so-called apostolic men hide failures in their relationships and in their ministries. Men will often hide their failures in their marriage and church relationships. Why? For fear of what others will think if they discover it. This, of course, is not God's way. Apparently, God is not afraid to reveal the failures of key men in Scripture such as David and Peter. Paul also revealed the relational breaches he had with Demas and Alexander the Coppersmith (2 Tim 4:10; 14). It is true that gossip is forbidden and that "where there is no wood the fire goes out" (Prov 26:20). The only reason to cover something is when it will damage another to reveal it. But is never right to hide things when those from whom they are hidden are part of the solution to the problem. Apostolic teams and church leadership must be open and above board with each other.

If our pride is not in the way and we are not trying to impress men then we have nothing to hide. If we are truly not subservient to the approval of men, then we will not be bothered greatly by their disapproval. Young men are actually strengthened by seeing leaders that are human, who occasionally fail, repent when humble enough to admit failure, and jump right up and continue. They are strengthened by seeing their leaders learning from their mistakes and continuing with Christ. This demonstrates the mercy and grace of our Lord. It demonstrates the humility of the leader and his dependence on the Lord. Authority is actually weakened when leaders hide their failures out of pride or fear of losing their position.

1 The Moral Compass, William J Bennett, Simon and Schuster, 1995, New York, NY, page 657.

2 If you think about it, it is also the basis of much false prophecy. The attempt at self glorification is present in some prophetic attempts. These go beyond what God has indeed authorized. As we approach the end, God must deal severely with false prophets. We must be found innocent of ambition when speaking for God.

# 13

# THE WITNESS OF THE APOSTLE'S LIFE

According to the grace of God which was given to me, as a wise master builder I have laid the foundation, and another builds on it. But let each one take heed how he builds on it. I Cor 3:10

## Wisdom

There are certain word groupings whose order is repeated throughout the whole of Scripture. These terms relate together and God wants us to see how they relate. For instance, mercy and truth are constantly related together with mercy always preceding truth (2 Sam. 15:20; Ps 25:10; 85:10, 86:15. 89:14; Pro. 3:3, 14:22, 16:6 and 20:28).

Similarly, wisdom and understanding are joined together throughout the entire Bible (Ex. 36:1; Deut 4:6; 1 Kings 4:29, 7: 14; 1 Chron. 22:12; Pro. 1:2, 2:6, 3:19, 4:5, 4:7, 8:1, 8:14, 24: 3; Isa. 11:2; Dan. 1:20, Col. 1:9).

Look at what the apostle Paul says about himself in 1 Cor. 3: 9-10:

> "For we are God's fellow-workers; you are God's field, you are God's building. According to the grace of God which was given to me, as a wise master builder I have laid a foundation, and another builds on it. But let each one take heed how he builds on it." (Emphasis mine)

Notice his reference to the wisdom that God had given him for building God's house. We shall see that wisdom is the chief characteristic that true apostles must have.

In the five-fold ministry the ministries of apostles and prophets are the key ministries necessary for foundational building. That is why they are always listed first and second in the two major lists of ministries in the New Testament (I Cor. 12:28, Eph. 4:11).

When these two "house-building" ministries are viewed in the context of another text from the Old Testament we are able to understand more fully each one's role in building God's house:

> "Through wisdom a house is built, and by understanding it is established. By knowledge the rooms are filled with all precious and pleasant riches." Prov. 24:3-4

Since God states clearly in this text that both wisdom and understanding are required to build a house, we can better understand what each (apostles and prophets) brings to the process. Since apostles are first in foundational building and wisdom is the chief element necessary in establishing a house, it stands to reason that wisdom must be the chief mark of an apostle while understanding that of the prophets. That is not to imply that an apostle has little or no understanding and the prophet has no wisdom. It simply means that a man who is a called apostle must demonstrate a consistent and unusual measure of wisdom. While wisdom alone is not the only characteristic of apostles, it is certainly the chief one.

What is the relationship between apostles and prophets with teachers? Another Scripture that might shed light on it is found in Proverbs 3:19-20.

> "The Lord by wisdom founded the earth, by understanding He established the heavens; By His knowledge the depths were broken up, and clouds drop down dew." (emphasis mine)

The prophet builds the walls of understanding and heavenly revelation. They keep out the enemy and keep in the knowledge that is poured into the house by the teaching gift. Only when apostolic wisdom and prophetic understanding are imparted into the foundations and walls, can they be safely filled with knowledge from the teacher. Only then can the rooms be filled with "all precious and pleasant riches" of good, house building teaching.

Knowledge "puffs up" (I Cor. 8:1) if it is not contained within the walls and foundation of wisdom and understanding. Many questionable doctrines are spewed forth in the myriad of books found today in Christian bookstores. Their veracity must always be measured and contained (or limited) by the walls built by wisdom and understanding. This explains why so many people and churches seem to drift off into humanism and strange doctrines as well as compromise. When an apostolic-prophetic foundation has not been laid, knowledge is not given the parameters it needs to be fruitful.

# Lifestyle

There are certain things we should know about a leader before we can have confidence in his or her leadership. The apostle Paul was not afraid to appeal to the things that his spiritual son Timothy knew about him as the evidence of his leadership:

> "But you have fully known my doctrine, manner of life, purpose, faith, longsuffering, charity, patience, afflictions, which came unto me at Antioch, at Iconium, at Lystra; what persecutions I endured: but out of them all the Lord delivered me" (2 Tim. 3:10-11).

It is not difficult, if you know what questions to ask, to ascertain a person's doctrine and basic approach to Scripture. This can be achieved rather quickly. On the other hand, it takes time to discern whether or not a person is living out what he believes or is hypocritical. Obviously, to "fully know" a person's manner of life, purpose, demeanor under crisis, stress, temptations, etc. as Timothy did Paul, it requires a relationship with that person.

The lifestyle and demeanor of a father-apostle figure is extremely important in identifying the legitimacy of his calling. It is interesting to note that the early church had drawn up a written code of conduct (called the 'Didache') by which churches could identify a true apostle or prophet. One of the first things the code dealt with was the issue of finances. If the so-called apostle or prophet personally asked for money it was considered as a sign that he was a false prophet or apostle.1 That is amazing, especially in light of the obsession many ministers seem to exhibit today regarding money. While poverty is clearly no blessing and the idea that a minister should live at a poverty level is ridiculous, for a man of God to leave the impression that he has come for money is wrong. Yet how many give the impression that their main motive is to collect money from God's people?

Paul certainly stresses in his letters that it is proper for churches to support apostolic ministry (2 Cor. 11:8-8, 1 Cor. 9:9-11, 1 Tim. 5:18). However when money becomes a motive for ministry it is a travesty. Paul reserved his severest rebuke in his letters for those who made this the motive for their ministry:

> "For the love of money is a root of all kinds of evil, for which some
> have strayed from the faith in their greediness , and pierced themselves
> through with many sorrows. But you, O man of God, flee these things
> and pursue righteousness, godliness, faith, love, patience, gentleness"
> (1 Tim. 6:10-11).

When this motive is operating it has the power to diminish and ultimately destroy relationships. That is why, in my opinion, the early church fathers included this warning about not receiving those who asked for money—they knew how potentially damaging such men would be to the church! In this light, we should always examine our own motives concerning money in the ministry.

The Scripture clearly says that God has set forth apostles (fathers) as last of all (1 Cor. 4:9-16). This should not be confused with his statement found later in the epistle that they are set as first in the church (12:28). The latter passage pertains to the place God has given the apostles governmentally in the church. Though they are first in government they are to be last in demeanor and presence, that is, in humility (and suffering). How much better off the church would be if true apostolic men could grasp this and learn to walk this tight rope, first in government, while being last in arrogance, covetousness, personal ambition, control, etc. Unfortunately, the history of the church testifies for the past two thousand years to the abuses of power and position that have taken place through church leaders who should have been fathers. The governmental authority side has been severely damaged by the general failure on the humility side. The result has been that many young leaders are afraid to fully submit themselves to apostolic oversight because of abuses they have seen or heard about and damaged relationships they have experienced. Fathers must strive to correct this so that the blessings can come upon young leaders and their churches.

Paul speaks in the above passage (2 Tim 3:10-11) about the persecutions he endured. This was a constant diet for these early apostles. Later, he reminds his son Timothy of the witness he maintained in these trials and how the Lord had delivered him out of them all. The question real apostolic fathers must face is, "What kind of face do we show the young men and our peers when the going gets really tough? Do we demonstrate faith when we walk through these trials?" This is clearly one of the qualifications for those who would be fathers in the faith. I imagine that the young men with Paul were greatly strengthened in their resolve to serve Christ when, after being stoned and left for dead, he got up and went right back to the city to visit the brethren (Acts 14:20).

In light of this we must be willing to ask ourselves some hard questions. What does it take to keep us from going forward for Jesus and His church? When we baby or protect ourselves or turn aside from fulfilling obligations because of inclement weather or personal inconveniences, what kind of message do we communicate to the younger men and to the church? Are we willing to endure hardness for the sake of the Gospel? Do we protect our health, privacy or comfort beyond obeying God and instead of fostering relationships in the Body of Christ? Are we able to go when tired or mildly sick? Some I have known will not reside with the saints on ministry trips, but insist instead on hotel accommodations. Does this work to foster and build relationships? We must be prepared to see our own difficulties as opportunities to strengthen the church. This is what Paul said about his sufferings in his second letter to the Corinthians:

"Now if we are afflicted, it is for your consolation and salvation, which is effective for enduring the same sufferings which we also suffer. Or if we are comforted, it is for your consolation and salvation. And our hope for you is steadfast, because we know that as you are partakers of the sufferings, so also you will partake of the consolation" (2 Cor. 1:6-7).

It is vital that younger men see stability and steadfastness in fathers. We cannot play-act but must actually express faith when things go awry. A dear brother once expressed it this way; "Aaron put on his beautiful garments when he went out before the people; he only had on his linen garment when before the Lord in the Holy of Holies." Before the Lord, in private, we are given the privilege of complaining and weeping. Many of David's psalms attest to this. However , we must walk in an attitude of stability, confidence, and faith before the people. If we don't possess and demonstrate faith and stability in times of hardship and crisis, it may be that in reality we are not called to apostolic ministry.

## Sowing Spiritual Things

In this regard, the apostle must exhibit utter purity in his dealings with finances. An apostolic father sows spiritual things, not material things (1 Cor. 9:11). This same Scripture allows him to reap material things, but not to sow them. It should cause great concern when we see purported apostolic men today drawing people and churches into business ventures and using kingdom relationships for sponsoring, promoting, and selling various things. The apostle must be very careful with even appearances of sowing material things into the church. While greed is rampant in our culture, it must not even be named among apostles as well as all Christian leaders. The Master laid down this basic axiom that one "cannot serve God and Mammon." We must never put ourselves in a light where people can for one moment feel as though we consider them prospects or customers instead of lovely sheep.

"Follow me as I follow Christ", Paul exhorted the Corinthians. I remember marveling at that statement when first reading it many years ago. At that time, I thought that Paul was either so far ahead of me that I would never catch up, or a supreme egotist. Yet as I matured, I understood that Paul was simply setting an example for the saints to follow. It is not, by any means, that Paul was perfect. But he was secure enough to know that to the best of his ability he was following Christ and therefore was not ashamed to ask men to follow him. At the end, he was able to say that he had run a good race and that a crown was laid up for him (2 Tim. 4:8). It should be the goal of every true father to be able to say the same thing.

## Attitude Toward Churches

The apostle represents Christ and is an extension of Christ's ministry on earth. Christ loves the church and died to give Himself for her (Eph. 5:25). The true apostle feels no less inclined to live and die in the same manner. That is certainly the heart of the apostle as witnessed by what he told the Corinthians:

"For I am jealous for you with godly jealousy, For I have betrothed you

to one husband, that I may present you as a chaste virgin to Christ"
(2 Cor. 11:2)

The apostle feels the jealousy that the Lord feels for His own
bride. That is not difficult to grasp. The best way to incur a man's
wrath is to molest his wife or fiancee. In ancient times, a king would
have eunuchs to care for his harem as well as his wives to insure
that their purity and chastity were preserved for the king. No one
dared to touch his intended bride with lusty or unclean hands. In
the same way, woe to those who touch the Bride of Christ with
unclean hands! The Lord is jealous over His bride and will judge
all who treat her improperly. As a father, the true apostle has this
same desire to see Christ's bride pure and spotless. He is jealous
for her in a godly way. The apostle Peter refers to those who by
covetousness exploit the saints (2 Peter 2:3). In the authorized version, this passage alludes to making merchandise of the saints. We
must watch our hearts and guard the flock in these last days against
those who would sully the bride.

Another aspect of the apostle's heart for the church is his willingness to "spend and be spent" for them (2 Cor. 12:15). He is
not the least bit concerned with recognition or achieving esteem at
the hands of the saints. While it is natural for a man to want to
be well-liked,  this cannot rule the decisions that a true apostolic
father makes. Sometimes to do what is right is not popular. To
serve the Lord and the churches, willing to be spent, even if there is
no immediate return, this has to be the heart of the apostle toward
the churches. His ultimate approval comes from God, not from the
people.

This has practical implications for the apostle's relationship to
the church and finances. Very often spiritual fathers demonstrate a
lack of integrity in this area. Some, while announcing that they live
by faith, are tempted to return to those larger churches  that give

the largest offerings. Are the smaller churches to be ignored? Are they to be loved the less or served the less?

It is possible for a man to have an 'intellectual' love for the church or the Body of Christ in general, and not transfer that love to specific churches in a practical way. There are many in this world who say they love the poor, but do not express that love practically to poor individuals on a one on one basis. The true father will base his ministry on the commands of the Holy Spirit and not on the size of the offering.

> "...besides the other things, what comes upon me daily: my deep concern for all the churches." (2 Cor. 11:28)

Paul penned these words to a church that was having trouble with his apostleship. He shows no signs however of holding back love or ministry to them even though they were rejecting him. Those who have ever had to minister to those who rejected them know how difficult it is. Paul's apostolic heart would not succumb to pettiness or let a spirit of rejection cause him to hold back. Though he be loved the less, he continued to look for any crack through which he could pour out his love.

> "Open your hearts to us. We have wronged no one, we have corrupted no one, we have cheated no one. I do not say this to condemn; for I have said before that you are in our hearts, to die together and to live together." (2 Cor. 7:2-3)

The apostle holds the church in his heart in the same way that a husband holds a wife in his heart. This should be expected if apostleship is just an extension of Christ Himself since that is exactly how He holds His Bride in His heart. It is grievous to the Holy Spirit when leaders look at the church as a pawn in a power game or a way to make a living and do not carry in their hearts the same concern for the church that the Lord Himself carries. While the Lord has never rejected the church for one moment, in a certain sense the church has rejected Him for the last two thousand years. Yet the Lord continues to love her regardless of her rejection. In the same way, leaders ought to love the church regardless of how they are treated by her.

## Bringing Joy to the Church

"But they shook off the dust from their feet against them, and came to Iconium. And the disciples were filled with joy and with the Holy Spirit" (Acts 13:51-52)

The apostles Paul and Barnabas were traveling. Proclaiming that the Gospel was being brought to the gentiles and being rejected by the Jews, they arrived at Iconium. Joy was the result of their visit. Joy should accompany an apostle, for joy is a fruit of the Holy Spirit and evidence of the kingdom. In one passage, Paul speaks of the joy that the believers brought to him (2 Cor. 1:14).

There should be joy and encouragement attending the ministry of the apostle. I have had the privilege over the years of hosting as well as attending many church gatherings where true apostolic team ministry was present and I have never failed in thirty years to see real joy accompany these meetings. Within a few days of this writing, I attended such a meeting where real apostolic team ministry was present. It involved a gathering of about twelve churches and their leaders and people. At least three apostles were present with the sole purpose of bringing encouragement and feeding. The times of praise and spontaneous dancing before the Lord were a testament to the real joy that was in that place. This should always occur when the true representatives of Christ tend to the flock. Fathers should bless the children. If we are to strengthen the churches, then joy has to be a result. The joy of the Lord is indeed our strength!

## Confidence in Christ

Beloved, if our heart does not condemn us, then we have confidence toward God. And whatsover we ask, we receive of him, because we keep his commandments, and do those things that are pleasing in his sight. And this is his commandment, that we should believe on the name of His Son Jesus Christ, and love one another, as he gave commandment.

1 John 3:21-23

The writings of the apostle John are absolutely unique in the New Testament. One of the reasons for the John's writings was to encourage confidence in God and His Son. As apostolic writings these letters reveal that at the heart of apostolic faith was utter confidence toward God inspiring one to believe in the Lord Jesus Christ.

When things go wrong, how quickly some apostolic leaders take matters into their own hands. Evidence that leadership is really mature is that it really believes and acts like Christ owns the church. Confidence in Christ is needed. This is one quality that must be evident in those who are apostles. They cannot be men who talk about God's sovereignty and grace on one hand and deny it entirely by the way they live and act. They must not manipulate men and churches for their own end. Their modus operandi is to pray, teach, preach, exhort, setting an example for others to follow. They must have utter confidence in Christ to move on hearts and bring about the desired goal. They must have this confidence to the end and believe that He will save to the uttermost.

Such confidence was evident in the apostle Paul who said:

"And we have confidence in the Lord concerning you, both that you do and will do the things we command you. Now may the Lord direct your hearts into the love of God and into the patience of Christ"

2 Thess 3:4-5 (emphasis added)

Paul's reference to commands never carries with it the idea of manipulation, but rather exhortation. The Greek root from which the word is derived means "to enjoin" or to "give a message." Many other Scriptures can be cited to show Paul's complete confidence in Christ's ability to move in His Church, His people, to accomplish His desired end. Paul's own ability to trust God and Christ was crucial to the success of his ministry. Seeing the apostolic father confident in Christ breeds confidence in the children as well. It is no wonder that he was able to transfer a measure of that confidence to the saints in the various churches as evidenced by the following Scriptures:

"And I wrote this very thing to you, lest, when I came, I should have sorrow over those from whom I ought to have joy, having confidence in you all that my joy is the joy of you all"

2 Cor 2:3 (emphasis mine)

"Therefore I rejoice that I have confidence in you in everything"

"And we have sent with them our brother whom we have often proved diligent in many things, but now much more diligent, because of the great confidence which we have in you.".

2 Cor 8:22

"I have confidence in you, in the Lord, that you will have no other mind; but he who troubles you shall bear his judgment, whoever he is"                                                                    Gal 5:10

"Having confidence in your obedience, I write to you, knowing that you will do even more than I say".

Phile 1:21

Paul's obvious confidence expressed to these churches should not be construed as confidence in human nature. Indeed, Paul had abundant experience to know the frailties of human beings and he was certainly not ready to trust them. Like His Master before him he also "knew what was in man" (John 2:24-25). Rather, Paul's confidence is in Christ and it is transferred to the elect because of his utter confidence that "he who has begun a good work in you will complete it until the day of Christ" (Philippians 1:6).

So often men preach publicly that Jesus will see them through and will never abandon them. Are they able to act it out? Unlike their Lord and Paul they do not exhibit the same faith toward the brethren. Will we have the same confidence in Him with regard to the church and God's purpose to sustain those that are His?

# Learn by Watching Dogs.

On more than one occasion I have had the privilege of watching a Scottish shepherd herd sheep with a trained sheep dog. The trained sheep dog achieves spectacular results by simply obeying the signals of the shepherd. This is a truly wonderful thing to watch. It is true that he has his own instincts and learns certain moves on his own within the parameters of his master's commands. I have heard of dogs actually running over the backs of the sheep to get to the other side of the flock in an emergency. Yet the sheep dog would never think of himself as the chief shepherd. His place is that of total obedience to his shepherd's commands. Having been with him since he was a pup, he has complete confidence that his master knows exactly what he is doing.

In a certain sense, apostles as well as leaders in general are to be like these sheep dogs. They are simply called to fully obey their Master's command regarding the Church. To be a true apostle there must be quiet confidence in the One who said, "I will build my church and the gates of hell shall not prevail against it!" (Matt. 16:18). The primary characteristic of a mature and godly leader is that he really believes that Christ is in charge. What is more, he acts like it as well. If he doesn't then he himself does not truly believe it and is therefore disqualified.

Part 5

•

# PASSING THE BATON

# 14

# THE ELIJAH-JEHU ANOINTING

In the Introduction we briefly mentioned the importance of the concluding prophecy of the Old Testament contained in the book of Malachi (4:1-6). This amazing prophecy sets the stage for the second coming of the Lord. It speaks of the sending of Elijah before the great and terrible day. Besides the specific promise of the return in glory of our Lord Himself, there is no more exciting prophecy in the entire Word of God.

The importance of this prophecy cannot be overestimated since it contains what might be properly called the "last words" of the Old Testament. If a man's last words are important, how much more the last words of God. A person will usually say something relatively important when speaking his final words to those he loves. In the same way, these final words of the Old Testament include some of God's most important thoughts

The heart of this prophecy is the promise of God to send "Elijah the prophet before the coming of the great and dreadful day of the Lord" who would "turn the hearts of the fathers to the children, and the hearts of the children to their fathers." In the Messiah's early history, contained in Luke's Gospel, we are clearly told how these words were amply fulfilled in the appearance of John the Baptist, whose coming was in the "spirit and power of Elijah (Luke 1:17). Yet the prophecy has important implications for the restoration of father-son relationships in the church today and for what we shall call the "Elijah anointing" and the resultant implications for spiritual warfare. We shall look at these aspects in this final chapter.

Our aim in this chapter is to underscore an important principle central to spiritual fatherhood; the need for spiritual fathers to understand God's plan and to have the ability to pass on that vision and have it implemented by their sons and grandsons. That is, while God raises up fathers who in turn are given great vision for the Church, they must not think that they themselves are to do it all. God's plan is for them to properly prepare the next generation so that when they are gone what they saw and lived for is being lived out in their spiritual sons. To understand this principle we shall look at the history of the prophet Elijah and the relationship he had with his spiritual son, Elisha who carried on his ministry after he was gone.

## Elijah Anoints Elisha

The story of Elijah and his amazing ministry is found in the book of First Kings. Elijah appeared at a time of great spiritual danger. The worship of Baal was rampant. Jezebel reigned with her husband Ahab. Elijah's ministry was to be mightily used to bring Israel back to the Lord their God. Yet many of the things he was told to do and longed to see in his lifetime did not occur. Rather, God reserved them for his spiritual son, Elisha to accomplish.

After Elijah defeated the prophets of Baal at Carmel he then fled from Jezebel who threatened his life. Passing through the wilderness, he came to Horeb, the mountain of God. There, God met Elijah and commissioned him to perform three tasks:

> "Then the Lord said to him: "Go return on your way to the Wilderness of Damascus; and when you arrive, anoint Hazael as king over Syria. Also you shall anoint Jehu the son of Nimshi as king over Israel. And Elisha the son of Shaphat of Abel Meholah you shall anoint as prophet in your place."
>
> 1 Kings 19:15-16

Looking at Elijah's later history we find that he only performed one of these tasks during his lifetime—anointing Elisha to be his replacement. This is quite amazing. At a time in his life when he felt like running from his duties, apparently losing his confidence in God, he was met by the Almighty, given the key to destroying the very enemy from whom he was running, and yet, he failed to carry it out. We would probably call him a failure today.

We know that God didn't look at it this way. Elijah later appeared on the Mount of Transfiguration with Jesus, which can hardly be construed as a reward for failure. James tells us that Elijah was a man with the same human frailty that we all have. It wasn't that Elijah had failed, but that God had simply desired that His 'spirit' be imbibed by a spiritual son who would in turn communicate that same spirit to other sons. Thus, the work of Elijah would be carried on to future generations.

Scripture is clear that Elisha actually received the mantle of Elijah as he saw him ascend to heaven in a whirlwind (2 Kings 2:11-12). As Elisha cried, "My father, my father, the chariot of Israel and the horsemen thereof", he took the mantle of Elijah and began to carry out his ministry.

## An Encouraging Prophecy

Many years ago I received a prophetic utterance from a man whom I respect very much. It stated that although I would produce a certain amount of fruit in my lifetime, my grandsons would produce a far greater amount of fruit than I.

One of my spiritual sons developed as an apostle in his own right in a foreign country. Several years elapsed and I had the thrill and privilege of visiting him on the field. As I watched him teaching the young students from remote mountain tribes in their native tongue, God spoke to me. Although I knew none of them personally, God witnessed to me in that moment that they were my grandsons. They were imbibing some of the 'spirit' that I had imparted to my son. Who knows what they will do for the Lord in their lifetime? I had a vision for this particular country, but I understood that I would never personally carry it out. We don't have to perform everything the Lord has let us envision! We can inspire those who can, our sons and grandsons.

## The Ministry of Elisha

That Elisha received Elijah's mantle is amply demonstrated by the fact that the two other tasks which God originally commanded Elijah to do were carried out by Elisha and his spiritual sons. Elisha anointed Hazael as king of Syria (2 Kings 8:7-13) and through his servant, he anointed Jehu as king over Israel (2 Kings 11:1-10). Thus, even though Elijah himself did not directly perform these acts in the person of his son he fulfilled all that the Lord had commanded him.

Reading the entire story of Elisha in the book of Second Kings we discover that the anointing on Elisha far exceeded that of his predecessor. Having received a 'double portion' of Elijah's spirit upon his ascension, he performed far more miracles than Elijah, not to mention that his ministry far outlasted that of his spiritual father. And in a sense, the young, unnamed son of a prophet who anointed Jehu was a spiritual grandson of Elijah. Thus, it is accurate to say that the Word of God traces at least two generations of spiritual sons of Elijah who imbibed his spirit, and fulfilled the original vision that God had given to their spiritual father.

What if Elijah had failed to anoint Elisha to succeed him? I think it is clear that without Elisha designated as Elijah's successor one of the most important spiritual victories in Israel would not have occurred. For it was in fact Jehu, another grandson whom Elisha anointed, who defeated Jezebel and thus fulfilled the vision of Elijah to rid Israel of her whoredoms and her controlling spirit (2 Kings 9:30-36).

Much has been written and preached of late concerning the spirit of Jezebel. This spirit manifests itself in many churches today as a spirit of rebellion and control whose aim is to emasculate all true authority in God's house. Elijah may have felt like he failed in his own day but God had a plan to use one of his own spiritual sons to carry out His purpose to rid the land of Jezebel.

Thus, the anointing upon Elijah was transferred to his son, Elisha, and then to his grandson, the young prophet who in turn anointed Jehu. It was this Jehu who destroyed the enemies of God and thus fulfilled the initial vision of Elijah.

## The Jehu Anointing

Jehu had a warrior's anointing to hate evil and stand up for good. How desperately needed this is today in the body of Christ. Not that we want to mirror Jehu completely, for this man produced much mayhem and carnage among the people. Nevertheless the heart and spirit of Jehu is desperately needed today in the church. It is an anointing for warfare to war against the enemies of God and defeat them.

Jehu also had another anointing which we need in the church today. He was indeed a warrior and a zealot. But he had something else. As he rode into town that day, Jezebel came out on a high balcony to meet him. She was attired in her seductive aura, beautiful in a worldly way. She was surrounded by several of her eunuchs (2 Kings 9:32). These eunuchs were by definition emasculated men. They were her servants. They were under her influence and control. She was a wicked queen. Do not forget that she had arranged the death of a man just to acquire a piece of land for her husband. She had inspired fear in the prophet Elijah. These eunuchs were hers to command.

But Jehu looked up and asked, "Who is on my side? Who?" The Holy Spirit then reveals that two or three of these eunuchs looked out on Jehu. Then Jehu commanded, "Throw her down!" They threw her down! Something powerful happened to these men. They were no longer under her control. They became men again. As they gazed at Jehu, a powerful anointing overcame them and changed them from eunuchs into activated servants of God. I call this the "Jehu anointing."

I believe that as the spirit of Elijah raises up and enables fathers to be real spiritual fathers in these days, and as they impart to their sons and grand sons the vision of the Coming King and His Kingdom, things will begin to happen. Not only will there be great warriors, but there will be those who will have the anointing to wake up the eunuchs in the church. Many men are asleep, emasculated if you will. When this anointing is manifested, men will begin to take their rightful places in families and churches.

## The Spirit of Elijah Today

The story of Elijah and the continuation of his ministry through his son Elisha has much instruction for us today. When most people talk about the spirit of Elijah they are referring to the miracles of this man of God and the many exploits which he did. And we certainly should, for this mighty man did many notable exploits.

Yet when Malachi refers to the appearing of Elijah before the Lord returns he does not refer to his miracles or mighty power but to his fathering ministry that would be evident. It is that aspect of this man's ministry that chiefly will characterize the days before the return of the Lord. We should expect that right up to the Lord's coming there will be a manifestation of Elijah's spirit "turning the hearts of the fathers to the children and the children to the fathers."

When fathers in our day begin to move in the spirit of Elijah, the results will be the raising up of powerful sons in their stead. The blessing of life mentioned earlier in this book will then flow from the fathers to these sons and daughters and hence into the church.

The anointing for warfare will also settle on the sons and daughters as well. What is God's purpose in this? One of things He intends to do is to use Elijah once again to destroy Jezebel in His house. We are obviously not talking about literal Jezebel since she has been dead and gone for centuries. Yet according to Scripture the spirit of Jezebel lives on in many churches and must be dealt with (Rev. 2:20).

## Conclusion

This completes our brief exploration into the subject of fathers. We have shown the importance and relevance of fathers and sons coming into divine alignment as the age closes. We have seen how true prosperity, blessing and life itself flows out of the correct and godly application of fatherhood to the church.

We explored some of the reasons fathers have made it so difficult for sons to properly relate to them and have shown what God would like to see as the heart of a true father. We have equated all of this to the emerging role of the apostolic ministry, which the Holy Spirit is releasing upon the earth today.

We have urged sons and daughters for their own sakes to relate properly to fathers even though those fathers may fall short. We cited the benefits that occur as a result of so honoring the principle of fatherhood. We showed that God loves fathers and causes life to come through them.

While trying to give a benchmark for young churches and leaders to measure against when sizing up men who call themselves apostles, at the same time it was the aim of this book to suggest that fathers ought to use the same benchmark to size themselves up. We should measure ourselves against the desires and guidelines of the Lord. Christianity is primarily a "heart" religion. What is in the heart is paramount to Christ. This should be our holy attitude for the sake of the Lord and His children. Everything is at stake! After all, didn't Malachi say, "and he (the spirit of Elijah) will turn the hearts of the fathers to the children, and the hearts of the children to their fathers, lest I come and strike the earth with a curse." The hearts are to be turned, not the functions or the positions. This book has majored on the aspects of the heart for that reason.

May the Lord turn all of our hearts more and more toward His great purposes as we see the day approaching. Holy Spirit, may you raise up many fathers in our day. Pour out the Spirit of Elijah on us all, for there are not many fathers!

Maranatha!

CPSIA information can be obtained at www.ICGtesting.com
Printed in the USA
BVOW04s1300180115

383830BV00001B/26/P